PRISONER OF WAR

PRISONER OF WAR

by

FRED HILL

Avon Books
1 Dovedale Studios
465 Battersea Park Road
London SW11 4LR

168 p.; 21 cm

30442

Printed and Bound in the U.K.
Avon Books London
First published 1994
© Fred Hill 1994
ISBN 1 897960 48 4

Foreword

by Ray Davey, former chaplain at Queens University, Belfast and founder of the Corrymeela Community.

It is for me a great pleasure and privilege to write this Foreword to Major Fred Hill's book. I can faithfully vouch for the authenticity of these stories from his life as a prisoner-of-war both in Italy and Germany after capture in Tobruk in North Africa in June 1942 by Rommel's Afrika Korps. We were captured together and shared life together in various camps for some 2 years. He represented the Salvation Army and I the YMCA. We used the opportunity of these years to proclaim the Gospel as, to use Paul's phrase "ambassadors in bonds."

I will never forget how Fred faced up to the ordeal of those years. He was considerably younger than I was – just 21 in fact. Yet he coped with all sorts of hardships – cold, hunger, overcrowded tents and huts, packed cattle wagons – with the greatest fortitude, humour and good temper. I never heard him utter an unkind word.

Fred witnessed to the Gospel of Christ day in and day out not only by his words but also by his music on the accordion which brought untold comfort and hope to multitudes of fellow captives, and also by the quality of his life, his patience, humility, sincerity and friendliness.

I do hope this book will be widely read as its message of hope and faith in the midst of adversity is very relevant today.

Ray Davey

Introduction

In the copious literature of the Second World War, this book has its own special interest.

The author, as a young Salvation Army officer still in his early twenties, found himself called to exercise his Ministry in a German Prisoner of War camp containing many thousands of men, who lived in small working camps spread over a large area of Saxony.

This book gives not only a vivid picture of what day to day life meant for these men and for himself, but also of what he saw of the life of the German civilian population on his travels, with a guard-interpreter, to visit these camps. His simple, detailed and often amusing account of his most unusual experiences makes fascinating reading.

Fred Hill's unique role often presented difficulties but, for him, difficulties were always opportunities for the exercise of his vigorous cheerfulness and irrepressible optimism. These, together with his sincere concern for others, were his distinctive characteristics, founded as they were on his indomitable Christian faith.

As one who was sustained by Fred's friendship at Hartmannsdorf for nearly a year, I warmly commend this book.

Rev. Richard H. Hill
Former Chaplain to the Forces

CHAPTER ONE
Prisoner of War
or
It Happened to Me

From North African Desert to Prisoner of War Camp

CHAPTER ONE
At the Edge of the Desert

I was in a hurry to get going. Two months at sea on a convoy dodging German U-Boats found me 'straining at the leash'.

Not that I disliked where I was, or what I was doing. In fact, there was never a dull moment at our Salvation Army Red Shield hostel, near the red-light district in the bustling city of Cairo during the Second World War.

There was plenty of activity. It was as if the world were putting on a non-stop show outside our hostel. Barrel-organs played noisily in the streets. Acrobats, strong men and even monkeys performed a few yards from where a cow was being milked. A patient donkey waited as milk was poured into churns slung across its back, ready for express delivery to the next customer.

There was colour, movement and plenty of noise. Motor horns competed recklessly for dominance of the highway. It provided a backcloth for the drama happening inside the hostel where up to 180 servicemen enjoyed the warmth of friendship and the luxury of clean white sheets, away from the monotony, danger and death of desert warfare.

I listened to their stories of action against Rommel's army in the North African desert. They had respect for the German general, bordering on affection. The desert battles were conducted in accord with 'civilised' rules of fairness and respect. The terrible atrocities happening in Western Europe came to light only at a later stage of the war.

Action was taking place not only on the battle field but

also in the minds and emotions of many young servicemen.

War can degrade. People are not only wounded in the body but also in the mind and heart. I listened to stories of inner conflicts, doubts about one's ability to cope, anxieties about loved ones far away, and the big question, what is the purpose of life? Some men attained heights of heroism and unselfishness which made an indelible impression on me, a mere 20- year old Salvation Army officer.

In this book I want to share with you what happened to some people during those days, how they reacted, how they changed; boys became men without losing their boyish sense of humour and adventure.

While waiting for my orders to leave Cairo I reflected on my short period of eighteen months as a Salvation Army officer.

The day the first air raid sirens sounded, found me shepherding pregnant mothers, and mothers with children under five years from the East End of London to the market town of Spalding. Sandbagging the Salvation Army's maternity hospital was my next assignment.

For six months I daily negotiated the cliffs of Dover with gallons of tea and a plentiful supply of cakes for men manning the huge coastal guns. It often coincided with the spectacle of heroic attempts by our fighter pilots to intercept German planes in the sky above.

Serving anti aircraft batteries and balloon barrage sites in the East End of London kept me busy for five months. But on many a moonlit night my canteen would race down the Mile End Road to the city of London. On one such occasion it was to witness the sight of the Salvation Army Headquarters at Queen Victoria Street engulfed in flames.

All I can say about that period was that I enjoyed the opportunity to be of service. It was exciting, it was interesting. If my friends had described me as happy but a bit superficial it would have been fair comment. I needed to mature.

But back to my opening statement: I was in a hurry to get going.

Yes, I certainly was, as I saw her standing outside the Salvation Army hostel in Cairo, immaculate and new. You could call it 'love at first sight'.

The object of my attention? A mobile canteen! Under the S.A. shield were the words, 'Presented by the Women of India'.

Major Fred Pearson, the officer in charge, beamed happily as he opened the cab door and handed me the keys. The call of the North African desert had come to me. Mine was to be the first British Salvation Army mobile unit to work with the Eighth Army.

A blast on the horn and away I went. North African desert, here I come!

CHAPTER TWO
On the Road

THE new engine purred reassuringly as I set out on my desert adventure.

It helped to have a reliable vehicle. I no longer had to lift up the bonnet constantly, as I did with the old Buick I drove during the London blitz.

From Cairo I motored to Alexandria – the gateway to the desert. The next day I set out for Mersa Matruh along the coast road, rarely getting into top gear because of bad road conditions. My instructions were to contact Captain Eric Saywell, the Eighth Army welfare officer, who would advise me where to operate my canteen.

Ruined town

After the drab monotony of the desert road it was breathtaking suddenly to come upon the wonderful blue of the Mediterranean at Mersa Matruh. I understand that Antony and Cleopatra loved to visit this popular Egyptian seaside resort, and bathe in the pool now named after that glamorous queen of the east. Today all holidaymakers had long since departed from this ruined town.

The only people in a holiday mood, despite their unshaven faces and stained dark green uniforms, were the Italian prisoners of war. They were relieved to be out of the fighting, preferring to sing and play guitars than to fight. Like many others they were caught up in a situation not of their own choosing.

I soon found myself talking to the tall, friendly Captain

Eric Saywell. We met in a sparsely furnished room in a derelict building which was the welfare department of the Eighth Army. He welcomed the Salvation Army reinforcement to the desert.

Gas mask

Before my departure the following morning Eric Saywell did everything possible to prepare me for life in the desert, remembering that for most of the time I would be living alone in the mobile canteen. Eric pointed out that I needed a gas-mask, and a tin helmet. He explained that I would require a shovel to dig the mobile canteen out of the sand, and he supplied me with the necessary equipment.

A mobile canteen in the open desert was an easy target for enemy fighter planes. I really needed a co-driver so that while one person drove, the other could sit on the top of the cab, looking out for enemy planes.

He wanted me to work with the 50th Division of the Eighth Army and said that many of the regiments were from Tees and Tyneside. Eric produced a set of ordnance survey maps and these were spread out on the floor. There seemed to be little or no red tape governing my movements, and the impression was that the desert was as much mine as anyone else's. I could go where I wished, although he drew a line on the map indicating it would be wise not to go beyond this boundary. Otherwise I might be captured.

I learned that, apart from a few coastal areas, towns didn't exist deep in the desert. But how would I know where I was?

That had been considered. 'Look there,' said Eric, indicating a point on the map. 'That is Piccadilly Circus, and further to the south is Knightsbridge.'

Seeing my puzzled expression he hastened to explain. Instead of the statue of Eros and neon signs there would be a pile of stones and petrol tins, on top of which there would be a sign, 'Piccadilly Circus'. That was it.

CHAPTER THREE
More Welcome than Leave!

FROM all sides of the desert they came; men in great haste, making for one central point. They came in tanks, armoured cars, lorries or on foot, but all had the same goal – me!

Out of the blue my Salvation Army canteen had arrived – a veritable movable oasis in the North African desert. As one panting Geordie runner reached the counter he exclaimed, 'You're more welcome than my leave!'

The journey had taken two days, mainly over rough desert tracks. There had been times when I thought the chassis and coachwork might part company. Vehicles don't last long in the desert. But I felt it had all been worthwhile as I looked at the animated faces of the men.

A guardsman put a one-pound note on the counter and simply said, 'Blow it.'

'But what do you want?' I asked.

'Just blow it,' he said with a grin. I think that had I turned up with a van of monkeys they would have bought them.

Many of the men queuing at the counter had known the movement and excitement of the earlier campaign when they were victoriously scampering across the desert. Then came the change of fortune when they scampered in the opposite direction. Now it was days of waiting, preparation and stabilisation. Gone were the high hopes of an early finish and a quick return home.

There was an additional worry about the future. In early

1942 England was still being heavily blitzed. Germany was victorious on all fronts and it looked as though the war could go on for 10 years.

Sandstorm

No place is duller than the desert when there is no relaxation or relief. When a sandstorm blows up, life is unbearable. Visibility is reduced to a few yards. The hot biting sand gets in your eyes, hair, ears and even into the food. Add to this the ever-present scourge of flies. Some units fortunate enough to be near the sea could break the monotony with a swim, but most were 20 or 30 miles south in the desert.

I wondered why so many men asked for a tin of health salts – but soon discovered it was to disguise the horrid taste of the drinking water. They also asked for writing material and magazines as these were unobtainable in the area.

Although our task was to provide material comforts there was another side of the work – meeting the emotional and spiritual needs of the men. It seemed easier to pray, or imagine the presence of God, in the desert.

A young artillery man wanted to talk about the recent death of his father. Another wanted to use the mobile canteen as a confessional. For others, life in the desert had begun to throw up deep questions about the purpose of life itself. The padre asked me to conduct religious worship, adding, 'Don't forget, plenty of singing and a good gospel address.'

The Bible shows that Jesus provided a constant example of how to meet both the material and the spiritual needs of people.

When he was helping an outcast, healing the sick and even feeding the hungry, he was also tuned into people's spiritual needs. His words, 'Man shall not live by bread alone but by every word that proceedeth out of the mouth of God', applied to life in the desert – and they apply to life today.

CHAPTER FOUR
Saved by Rifle Shots

HOW would you react if someone fired a rifle at you as you were driving your car?

When this happened to me my first impulse was to put my foot harder on the accelerator. But I looked again at the man and had second thoughts. He might *not* be an enemy soldier – everybody looked the same in the desert, dressed in shirt, shorts and forage cap. I decided to stop.

The man firing the rifle ran breathlessly up to the mobile canteen and gasped, 'Don't move, don't even turn round! I've fired three shots over your head – the next one was to go through your engine. It might have got your legs, but it would have been worth it. You're driving straight into a minefield. You would have been blown up and almost certainly killed.'

Trip-wire
It was only then that I noticed the trip-wire about four inches from the ground indicating the beginning of a minefield.

The British soldier with three stripes on his arm explained that he was on patrol in no man's land. I thanked him profusely, offering him a tin of pineapple or anything else he wanted from the canteen. I backed the canteen very carefully away from the trip-wire, changed direction and headed for safety.

It was only as I was driving away from the sergeant and the minefield that the full force of the incident began to dawn on me. I began to hold a conversation with myself that I had come very near to being killed. It didn't seem real and took some time to sink in.

Coincidence

As I sped to safety I wondered what God had to teach me through the incident. Was it just a strange coincidence that, at the exact time I was heading for the minefield, the sergeant was at that particular spot? I wondered too what the sergeant felt about the experience. But that seemed just idle speculation because I didn't know his name, or where he lived in England, and I was unlikely ever to meet him again.

But life is full of surprises. The question has now been answered by former Sergeant Eric Moult, for that, I now know, is the name of the desert sergeant.

Forty-three years after the event Eric Moult wrote to *The War Cry* asking what happened to the Salvation Army officer whose life he had saved. I haven't yet had the pleasure of meeting Eric but we have corresponded.

Eric wrote to me recently about 'coincidence'. 'I did not just happen to be on that spot, Fred. If I tell you my own experience, you will realise the Lord's part. I believe God wanted a minister in the prisoner-of-war camps – and you had to be the one person.'

Eric is proving from his own past experience that God works out his purpose in the lives of those who are open and responsive to his will. It is a great way to live, and it certainly simplifies life.

Future

This truth is beautifully expressed in one of the choruses I sing in The Salvation Army.

I'm in his hands, I'm in his hands;
Whate'er the future holds, I'm in his hands.

The days I cannot see have all been planned for me;
His way is best, you see,
I'm in his hands.

CHAPTER FIVE

Broken Springs but no Bullet Holes

IT was just another uneventful night, although the twinkling stars and the vast stillness of the desert induced a sense of wonder. I slept soundly and peacefully on some packing cases in my mobile unit.

'Thank God there's no sandstorm,' I thought on opening the back door next morning. I stretched, took a couple of breaths of desert air and felt that life was good. After shaving, then pouring petrol on some sand to heat water to make a cup of tea, I set out to serve the men of the 50th Division. I hoped my visit would be a welcome break from the monotonous routine for the men from Tees and Tyneside who had spent months just waiting for something to happen.

'Don't you know the battle has started?' said a corporal with a Tyneside accent, as I stopped my mobile canteen at a front-line position. 'What - *the* battle?' I asked. 'The battle we've expected for months?'

'The lads will be pleased to see you,' he added, with a voice betraying some nervous excitement, 'but you can't stay long because we are about to close the gap, then no one can go in or out.'

Event

As a defensive measure the regiment had surrounded itself on all four sides with minefields, the idea being that in the event of an enemy attack, the regiment would not retreat but continue to fight – until the last man, the last round of ammunition. At least, that was the theory.

As soon as I opened the serving hatch, the various comforts I had brought were distributed in record time to men whose minds were focused on what might happen to them in the next few hours. Nervousness, excitement, fear, anxiety, numbness and a sense of relief that, at last, something was going to happen, made a cocktail of emotions expressed in a variety of ways. There were tense, nervous movements, laughter, bravado, and quiet withdrawal.

I promised that if possible I would see them again. With the words 'Hope things go all right', I was away through the gap in the minefield just as the corporal and his men were about to bury the land-mines and shut the gap.

'That's strange,' I thought as I drove from the front line. 'The corporal said the battle had started but the air isn't filled with exploding shells or the crack of riles.' The mystery was solved when I reached the rear divisional headquarters many miles behind the front line.

Soldiers had taken up positions in slit trenches and I was told that a tank battle was in process. 'How ridiculous,' I thought, 'to be in a tank battle and not to know!' A soldier from the Durham Light Infantry, holding a molotov cocktail ready to throw at an enemy tank, pointed to an escarpment about a mile away. Tanks which I had assumed were British were, in fact, German.

Nearly fifty years later, Frank Kitchener, former editor of the "Observer", gave his impression of that occasion: 'We had had a tough day, with the German Afrika Korps belching out its shells at us with its vastly superior armour, and so had the Germans.

We both withdrew a little way, almost as if by agreement.

My "buddy" and I were in adjoining slit trenches on the leeward side of our tank. The Germans were not content to leave it at that for a time. Their artillery had our range and shells were sporadically dropping among us. Not a barrage, but uncomfortable nevertheless.

Then, as we sheltered and rested, my mate suddenly said, "What the 'ell's this?" A van stopped. The driver got out, pulled down the side of a shutter and shouted, "Come on, lads. We're open for business. The Salvation Army's here."

We climbed out of our shelter and stood in a line. There were sweets, pineapple chunks and cigarettes. Where the van came from, and how it got to our front line, we could not know. Then, having sold up, the Salvation Army man shouted, "Cheerio, lads, keep smiling."

There was no need to describe our morale after that. We learned later that this Salvation Army man received a well-deserved decoration.'

Chaos

Apparently at midnight General Rommel's tanks had crept south into the desert, by-passed the British forward positions and come up behind the Allied lines causing chaos.

As the wide open spaces of the desert provided no hiding place I drove as fast as I could away from the scene of the action.

I hadn't gone far before receiving the attention of the German tanks. The shells and machine-gun fire I had expected in the morning had been saved for the afternoon performance.

Without bullet holes, but with two broken springs, my mobile canteen limped back to the relative safety of Tobruk.

I left behind two tank regiments, still slogging it out. In one of the tanks was a British tank commander. He was a young man who immediately gave the impression of being special; he just seemed to have everything – physique, intelligence, charm.

Soon after the battle, in which tanks with no cover had

stood and tried to blow each other to pieces, he spoke of what it was like and how he hated it all. He spoke also of his deep Christian faith, and of the overwhelming longing he had, just to get out of his tank and go across and shake hands with the German tank commander.

Christians, like others, have to live in a complicated world where choices have to be made. The choice is not always between good and evil, which is fairly simple, but between the lesser of two evils. To stand aside while a weaker person is ill-treated is wrong, but to use physical force against the aggressor may also seem to be wrong.

As a Christian the young tank commander could not contract out of life. He had to make decisions and take responsibilities. Nevertheless he retained a strong faith in God and a love and respect for the person on the opposing side.

CHAPTER SIX
To Pit a Rifle Against a Plane

WHAT a relief to arrive back to the relative safety of Tobruk where the Royal Army Ordnance Corps would repair the broken springs of my canteen!

Let me give you a picture of Tobruk as I saw it. The town stood on a narrow peninsula and was built on hard yellow rock. Of course, there was the breathtaking blue of the Mediterranean, but the harbour and bay were already the graveyard of 30 ships, some of whose decks, masts and funnels were still visible.

Apart from a few stunted palm trees nothing seemed to grow in Tobruk and any civilians had long since departed. Tobruk, later featured in a war film bearing its name, was a well-tried veteran of war, as I was soon to discover.

On my first arrival at the town centre, impressions came with dramatic suddenness. It seemed that suddenly everything was going up or coming down; as German Stuka planes dive-bombed and strafed, everyone with a weapon, from an ack-ack gun to a rifle, was firing back. To pit a rifle against a plane was a pretty futile effort, but the psychological gain of everyone 'having a go' seemed to boost morale tremendously.

Almost as soon as the raid started, it was over – probably it lasted no more than a minute. Not one building in the town had escaped damage!

Escaped
Yet, in a strange way I felt safe in Tobruk. Like a homing

pigeon I seemed to find my way back to Tobruk once every four days. To be part of a friendly Christian community, where I could relax, more than compensated for the physical danger. I learned that emotional and spiritual security is more important than physical and material security.

A sight that did catch my eye in Tobruk was the Salvation Army red shield sign on the wall of one of the buildings. Although I was the first British red shield officer to operate in Tobruk, our Australian Salvation Army officers had arrived before me. They had the distinction of operating during the nine months' siege of Tobruk.

The way in which the Aussies defended Tobruk during the siege is an incredible story. It was recounted that they would go out on night patrols to pinch enough guns and ammunition from the enemy to defend the garrison. The carefree 'happy-go-lucky' Aussies, with their slouch hats, would think nothing of approaching an enemy tank and shoving an iron bar between the tracks to immobilise it, or even climbing on the back of a tank and waiting for the turret to open.

The Aussies were brave, sometimes reckless – but if ever I was in a spot of danger or difficulty I couldn't do better than have an Australian mate.

I was very moved to see that outside the town was a war cemetery with hundreds of graves, mostly of Australian soldiers.

CHAPTER SEVEN
Things Begin to Hot Up

TO me, people are more interesting and important than places. So I cannot think of Tobruk without recalling the men I met.

Harold Barker who came from Herne Hill, South London, had a charismatic personality. For his work as a YMCA secretary in the nine-month siege of Tobruk he was awarded the MBE. His citation read:

'Despite bombing and the unusual hardship of the siege, he remained at his post, showing self-control and calm courage. He has been at all times untiringly cheerful and ready to serve in any way possible.'

As I worked mainly alone with my mobile canteen, I made the Tobruk YMCA my base when returning from trips into the desert. It was good to share friendship with other Christian workers even though I didn't always appreciate Harold's light-hearted 'Rise and shine!' accompanied by the crashing of a biscuit tin on the concrete floor of the store room in which we slept.

He possessed the art of combining an easy, happy manner with strong Christian principles. Harold Barker's 'swear box' was an illustration.

Directed

A crowd of British soldiers is likely to compete with any other nationality – with the possible exception of the Aussies – when it comes to swearing. Any newcomer to the canteen caught swearing was immediately directed to Barker's 'swear box' on the counter. Amid great laughter his mates would make him pay up half a piastre or 'acker', the smallest Egyptian coin. Because of the friendly atmosphere engendered by Harold no one ever thought of objecting.

As I got to know Harold I realised that his courage and complete unselfishness stemmed from a strong Christian faith.

During June 1942 the desert battle began to 'hot up' and it was difficult to keep track of the units I served. The situation was fluid and fast moving.

'Is it safe to go along this track?' I enquired of a signal unit.

'We don't really know,' replied the sergeant in charge, 'but let us know when you come back.' He didn't know any more about the state of the battle than I did!

Besieged

Later that day I parked on a junction outside Tobruk where I issued free comforts to servicemen who were about to break out from the encircling movement of the German Army.

Many years later, Eric R. Moss from Oxford recalled the subsequent retreat: 'I remember that terrible retreat of the Eighth Army to El Alamein, and I also remember the only vehicle going towards the enemy that I saw during those long hours sitting in our lorry. That vehicle was a Salvation Army van which brought forth shouts of admiration and thanks from the disconsolate men with me.

The only army going towards the enemy was the Army of Christ. I salute you and the soldiers of your army' Eric Moss.

On my return to Tobruk I was ordered to report to the brigadier in charge of the Tobruk garrison. He explained that Tobruk was likely to be besieged again and in the event of an evacuation by sea it wouldn't be possible to include my mobile canteen. Having heard the many exciting stories about the previous siege I felt a sense of privilege to be of service at such a time.

So we prepared for the siege. I was to take up quarters with the YMCA. My mobile unit would be used to visit the servicemen defending the perimeter; a piano would also be installed in it to aid the conducting of sing-songs and religious services. In two days' time we were to meet the senior padre to plan the details of the welfare work to be undertaken during the siege. There was an air of excitement and adventure.

Next morning we awoke to a more-than-usual amount of attention from the attacking forces. In addition to the Stuka raids, artillery shells were dropping uncomfortably near. There was a feeling around that something was about to happen, but what?

CHAPTER EIGHT
Captured!

WE decided to white-wash the canteen building on one of the most fateful days of our lives.

'That was a near one,' exclaimed Ray, as we all instinctively bent our knees and crouched as if to dodge the latest shell flying to its destination.

Things had certainly begun to happen – and we wanted to know about it. Someone stepped down from the plank to switch on the BBC news. The announcer said that it was doubtful whether the Germans were going to attack Tobruk as the Eighth Army was strong enough to hold them. Later that morning Harold Barker went down to the Area Headquarters and came back with the reassuring news that everything was 'well in hand'.

The one thing we were certain about was that we were filthy dirty. So we agreed to make a dash for Anzac Cove to bathe in the sea. We piled into the 15-cwt truck, passing through strangely deserted streets. No sooner had we begun to luxuriate in the lovely waters of the Med than we were aware that across the bay vehicles and stores were becoming enveloped in a mass of fire.

Then we were aware of things dropping in the water around us as if someone was throwing stones. It dawned on us: it was a creeping barrage from guns on the opposite side of the bay! Drying ourselves in record time we dashed for the truck and drove back to the canteen.

It was 7 pm, and although the shelling had ceased, Ray, who later became chaplain of Queen's University, Belfast, decided to go and find out what was happening. He put his head out of the door and quickly returned, looking pale.

'There are some German paratroopers coming up the road,' he said. (They were actually infantry but he thought they were paratroopers.) They were firing indiscriminately and throwing grenades into buildings as they proceeded along the road.

Without time to collect a toothbrush we found ourselves with our hands above our heads, filing out of the building into the street battle which was in progress. As we were lined up against a wall a tank trundled down the road towards us. To look down the barrel of a tank gun is a strange experience. I just hoped that the man inside the tank wasn't 'trigger-happy'. Panzer troops arrived and took up positions at street corners.

Ridiculous

We stood with our hands above our heads. One of my friends said, 'What about your accordion, Fred?' When I think about it now it seems ridiculous that I should actually go up to one of the German soldiers, in the middle of the street battle, and ask if I could return to the building to collect my piano accordion.

We couldn't speak each others' languages, so I pointed to 'Salvation Army' on my epaulette and indicated that I needed to go back into the building. To my surprise he followed me. When he realised it was a canteen he looked at me with a question mark on his face and said 'Beer?' – apparently a universal word. I shook my head, hoping he would not take a dim view of the situation.

When I showed him the accordion he indicated that I must leave the case because I would be marching a long way. With my accordion on my back and my hands still above my head, I joined my friends as we were marched through the streets to a central square, to be joined by hundreds of other prisoners of war.

During our march through the street, one German soldier, in combat position at the corner of a street, shouted, 'It's a long way from Tipperary now, Tommy!'

At the end of the battle there was no enmity or hatred on either side. The attitude of the Germans towards us was, 'We've won, you've lost, better luck next time.'

At that particular time I might have likened the post-battle period to the friendly rivalry of players and fans at the end of an English football match. Unfortunately, because of events in recent times, the analogy of the English football match is no longer valid.

CHAPTER NINE
Caged

'WHAT a transformation a couple of hours has made!' I thought as we reached the town centre with many other prisoners of war. Lights were shining in what was formerly the Area Office of the British Command. German soldiers were playing around with captured motor cycles and cars to see how they worked.

'Look,' exclaimed a fellow prisoner of war, 'there's your canteen.'

Sure enough, my canteen with its Salvation Army red shield sign on the side, and the notice explaining that it had been donated by the women of India, was being driven down the road by a German soldier.

Gone were the days when that canteen would operate as a dispenser of comforts, a pulpit or a confessional. No longer would young servicemen, seeking new courage and strength, kneel and pray to God in that canteen. The canteen, which had served as my home for six months, disappeared down the hill.

Our captors showed no particular jubilation. Although efficient, they seemed tired and stood around smoking and chatting, not unlike any crowd of British soldiers.

An hour later, when it was getting dark and cold, we were moved to the hospital compound where we spent the night under the stars. Sleep didn't come easily as our minds raced over the events of the past hours and the uncertain prospects for the future.

Wounded

Next morning I watched the wounded of all nationalities being brought into the hospital. German and British doctors worked together and I noted that the injured from both armies lay side by side and were treated in strict order, regardless of nationality. As I witnessed the pain and suffering, I realised how fortunate I was to have escaped injury.

While hanging around the hospital compound the next day we came upon a quartermaster's store and quickly obtained such things as shaving kit, tooth brush, a blanket, a groundsheet and one spare shirt to be shared between Harold, Ray and myself. For many months that shirt rotated between us when each decided to wash his own shirt.

The other acquisition was a New Testament which also became common property and which played an important part in our work in the prison camps. I still possess that copy of the New Testament.

From the hospital compound, housing hundreds, we were taken to an improvised prisoner of war cage on the El Gubi drome, just outside Tobruk, where there must have been between 15,000 and 20,000 prisoners – a most depressing sight.

Although brief it was one of the worst experiences of our captivity. A horrible khamsin, which is a hot south or south-east wind which blows during that part of the year, was active.

Shelter

Imagine yourself in front of the open door of a hot oven, with heated sand beating into your face under pressure. With no tree, shrub or tent to offer shelter, my only ambition was to hide my face from the sand-storm for a few seconds and to obtain some water.

Fortunately, after two hours came the order that all

officer personnel were to move. I found myself in a truck with officers mainly from the Brigade of Guards, including Bill Bowes, the famous Yorkshire cricketer.

As the sun poured down on our truck-load of prisoners, I thought about our unknown future. Not only about the possible adventures and dangers which might befall us, but also about that inner world which we all inhabit, whether we are religious or not. Soon all philosophies and faiths – or the lack of them – would be put to the test.

A few weeks prior to our capture, Harold Barker and I had spent a part of Easter week in Jerusalem. Like Jesus' disciples we had made the pilgrimage to the Mount of Olives. In the company of others we had sung a hymn and prayed. Although sincere, the disciples were still immature; regarding spiritual things they were still 'thick'.

We too were sincere, and I felt inexperienced and not greatly fitted for the challenge of the future. Would my Christian faith stand the test? I had yet to prove it.

CHAPTER TEN
The Bayonet in my Back

I SIGHED with relief! It was still there – the linen bag full of money, tucked inside my shirt, attached to string around my neck. The German soldier who had searched me, after I had been taken prisoner, failed to find it.

But that was three days ago. In the meantime I had been handed over to Italian soldiers, which meant another search. A diminutive Italian corporal conducted the search as we all lined up in single file.

Ray, standing next to me, tried to remove his wrist watch and transfer it to a pocket. A guard whose covetous eyes had spotted it told the corporal, who yanked Ray out of the ranks. When Ray remonstrated and asked to see the commandant he received a slap on the face. I was relieved that Ray, a former Irish international rugby player, managed to keep his temper in check as another guard was at his back with bayonet drawn and ready.

It was my turn next. I couldn't hide a piano accordion in my pocket. The corporal drew another guard's attention to the Italian name on the accordion, apparently indicating he had more right to it than I had. I was sad to see it go, but a bayonet in the back is quite a forceful point. However, I still retained the linen bag.

What was important about the linen bag? The piano accordion I'd just lost was mine – it belonged to me; but the contents of the linen bag belonged to The Salvation Army. I felt a sense of responsibility, of accountability. I wanted the satisfaction of returning it to its rightful owner – The

Salvation Army – even though the Army headquarters had no idea I possessed it. The manner in which I hid the bag over three years as a prisoner, involving many searches, is an interesting story. I have space to recount just one incident.

Two-and-a-half years after my arrest I had been transferred to a German headquarters camp where I lived in a room with 16 other British prisoners. Suddenly the door opened and a German voice shouted, 'Everybody, get out!'

It was another lightning search. Sometimes it was for clandestine electric cookers. At other times knives, escape equipment or money were the target. I protested that, as the Salvation Army chaplain, I should be allowed to remain, to ascertain that the search was conducted properly. They agreed to this request.

'Search the bags!' ordered the officer, pointing to the racks at one end of the room.

My heart sank. There on the rack was my kit bag containing my linen bag and its contents. Kit bags and boxes were being taken from the rack and placed in a pile. After being searched they were transferred to another pile.

Then an inspiration came! I moved forward, and began helping the guards by placing bags on the pile, then moving them to another pile when they had been searched – making certain that the two piles got closer! Then came the moment when I brought down my own kit bag and placed it at the edge of the pile. As the guards suddenly focused their attention on a knife which had been found, my right foot quickly pushed my bag towards the pile which had been searched.

It was a happy day for me when, after three years in captivity, I placed my linen bag on the table of The Salvation Army's National Headquarters in London, and could say, 'Here it is. I haven't lost any of it.'

Here on the table were my canteen takings during the time I worked in the desert. In that brief moment I was probably the most popular person in The Salvation Army! In those days, £700 was a considerable amount of money. I had been the steward of that money; it didn't belong to me. It was a thrill to hand it back.

Just as The Salvation Army entrusted me with that money, so God has entrusted me with my life. It doesn't belong to me; it belongs to God. Will I experience a similar thrill when I eventually come into God's presence and give an account of how I have used the gift of life which God has given me?

To live life with a sense of accountability to God is a marvellous experience. It means that we are important in the sight of God. That gives a sense of self-worth and dignity.

CHAPTER ELEVEN
Flight to Italy

AS the Italian Savoia aircraft gained height we said goodbye to the North African desert. It was an ideal day for the journey. The sky was cloudless and the sun very strong, almost as if the desert was putting on its best appearance for our departure.

Through the aircraft window I could see the Benghazi compound where thousands of Allied prisoners were making an effort to survive. Probably at that moment watches, wedding rings, and even boots were being bartered with Italian guards across the barbed wire in exchange for some water. The joke went round, 'Shut your mouth when you sleep otherwise the guards will pinch your false teeth.'

Many men were suffering from dysentery with no hope of medical treatment. Life was precarious. One prisoner in a playful mood, observing a guard patrolling on top of a wall, had made a noise like a cat. He was shot dead.

There was a striking contrast between the treatment of officers and other ranks. We were being conveyed to Italy by plane instead of being battened down in the hold of a ship.

Welfare

Many of the men in that Benghazi camp were to spend months in those conditions before being transported in overcrowded ships, without proper sanitation, with many of them still suffering from dysentery.

Before boarding the plane I had been officially registered as a prisoner of war. Although I had the status of a military officer and wore officer's uniform, I was officially a civilian, seconded to the Eighth Army for welfare work.

When I stepped up to the table to be registered I tried to explain my position. A puzzled expression came over the face of the interviewing officer.

'But what is your regiment?' he inquired.

'I belong to The Salvation Army,' I replied.

'But you must belong to a regiment,' he insisted.

I could only repeat what I had previously stated. He wiped the perspiration from his forehead and, as if he had suddenly cleared his mind, the answer came. He picked up his pen and wrote beside my name 'Salvation Army Grenadiers'.

Back in the plane, everybody, including guards and aircrew, seemed tired. The wireless operator, putting on his earphones, appeared to adjust the controls. Smoke poured from the set, so he casually took off the earphones and didn't bother with them again.

Sitting next to me on the plane were Ray Davey and Harold Barker, the two YMCA secretaries with whom I had been captured.

Water

Harold, a much older man, was an inspiration to Ray and myself. I learned much from him regarding living a victorious Christian life. Being concerned about the plight of the 'other ranks' who were without water, Harold nearly missed the plane. With a quiet conviction and authority he had persuaded parties of officers to carry water from our barracks – where there was an adequate supply – to the compound where men were needing water to survive.

Ray, Harold and myself were to remain together for another 18 months. Harold was a Church of England layman, Ray a Presbyterian minister and myself a Salvation

Army officer. Denominational differences seemed irrelevant; we were all part of the body of Christ, called to love and serve others.

During prison life Ray, who came from Ireland, was developing convictions about Christian community. Later he became chaplain of Belfast University, and then became the founder of the well-known Corrymeela Christian Community in Ireland, dedicated to reconciliation and peace.

Had he not been a prisoner of war and experienced the love and unity between Christians of different denominations, he might not have caught the vision.

His life proved that, if we are open to God, every experience, no matter how grim, is an opportunity to know more about him and his will for our lives.

CHAPTER TWELVE
He Killed Because of Fear

AS I alighted from the Italian aircraft which had brought us across the Mediterranean to the town of Lecce in the heel of Italy, I counted my blessings. I was still alive, not wounded and had some good friends. I can face anything when supported by friends.

As a bonus I had been given my first pay. I spent it the following day on plums and sweets during the journey from Lecce to Bari, which we made in a first-class railway compartment. We were escorted by the Bersaglieri, a very smart Alpine regiment, wearing Alpine boots and Robin Hood cocked hats, complete with a long grey feather.

On the way we had a long stop at the crowded port of Brindisi. As we waited at the station someone had a glance at a German newspaper which contained headlines we could all understand – 'Mersa Matruh Gefallen'. Things were obviously going badly for the Allies in the Middle East.

We spent the first night in the Bari transit camp in the relative comfort of bungalows. We expected to be there for a few weeks.

Transferred

But then our situation drastically changed. Ray and Harold were to be transferred from the quarters for those of officer status to that of 'other ranks'. I decided to go with them as I would be of more service in an 'other ranks' camp than in an officers' camp. I soon experienced the vast difference between life as an officer and that of 'other ranks' in captivity in Italy. Immediately we went from a bungalow to a flimsy, poorly pitched tent in a small compound about 70 by 40 yards – more like a chicken run – with an odd assortment of humanity. There were Cypriots, Greeks, Jugoslavs, Jews, Arabs, Russians, Australians, New Zealanders, South Africans and Britons.

The two Australians and two New Zealanders were the most resourceful fellows one could ever meet. They had lived a rough life in Greece for over a year, hiding from the enemy before being captured. They made the best of everything and had no use for self-pity or insincerity. One of them had worked for a Greek farmer and had learned the language fluently. On several occasions he had sold water-melons to the occupying German forces.

While we were at Bari a group of prisoners arrived from North Africa after a horrible trip across the Mediterranean in the hold of a ship. Many were in bad shape. One of these lads arrived suffering severely from dysentery. On his way to this tent he was not sure of his bearings, wanting only to flop down in any corner.

Frightened

At 2 pm he staggered out of his tent to make his way to the latrine, but ended up at the barbed wire perimeter. The guard, about 10 yards away, became frightened, probably thinking he was trying to escape. He lifted his rifle and killed him instantly.

These Italian guards were not brutal or arrogant, but very frightened of their prisoners. A man who is frightened is very dangerous, particularly when he is armed. Fear is usually the result of ignorance. The guard was ignorant of the reason why the prisoner was near the barbed wire. He probably fantasised that he was about to be attacked; fear and panic took over with fatal results.

Much violence, whether it involves countries, families or individuals, is the result of fear, arising out of ignorance or misunderstanding. The partners in a marriage may be charming, pleasant, and certainly not violent people, yet because of fear and misunderstanding they can end up doing violent things to each other.

If anyone eventually presses the button to set off a nuclear weapon, it will most likely be because of fear and panic.

CHAPTER THIRTEEN
Home is a Groundsheet

IT'S six weeks since we put our hands up at the battle of Tobruk. We are on the move again – we hope we're going to our permanent camp. But we have come down in the world – no more travel by air or first class on the railway!

We left Bari in cattle trucks, although not before being subjected to yet another search. This time they took papers, notebooks, photos, knives, forks and enamel mugs.

We began to feel like plucked chickens; there wasn't much more they could take from us. We had been issued with an aluminium dixie for our 'skilly', but this was withdrawn for the 'war effort', and in its place we were given an earthenware pot which quickly broke. At least we still retained our spoon.

After a 24-hours' journey we arrived at Lucca, very near to the leaning tower of Pisa. It was part of the Dante country and the little hill beside the station was mentioned in one of his poems. But our thoughts were not of the beautiful scenery. We wanted sight of our next 'home'.

Fantastic yarns

The most fantastic yarns had circulated. Someone even told of a prisoner writing home requesting suitable clothes to go to a dance. Many of us had a picture in our mind of a representative of the International Red Cross at each camp. Would there be decent huts in which we could live?

At last we came upon the now familiar barbed wire and sentries mounted on platforms. But where were the buildings, our homes for the future? Our homes were handed to us as we went through the gap in the barbed wire. Poorly clad Italian guards, with buttons off their uniforms, rags for socks and broken bootlaces gave two pieces of groundsheet measuring six feet square to every four men. Try as we might, it was humanly impossible to get four bodies under those two pieces of groundsheet. However, by joining all our sheets together we were able to make long low tents with the fronts permanently open to accommodate all the bodies. There were no groundsheets to lie on.

What did please us was the sight of a crop of dandelions growing in the field. They quickly disappeared because the men were desperately hungry. Some even tried to eat grass, but found this impossible.

A group of prisoners arrived from another camp and told us they had been sent to our camp as punishment for building a tunnel. We were not surprised that we were in a punishment camp.

Barbed wire

After erecting our tent I went for a walk around the compound. I looked at the barbed wire, and then at the countryside beyond it. I thought of home. I wondered how many years I might be incarcerated in this camp. As if I had suddenly been hit by a brick, the full significance of being a prisoner dawned on me.

Until this point there had been excitement – being taken prisoner, various transit camps in the desert, fantasies about dramatic rescues. Even when flying in the plane across the Mediterranean, the thought that the crew might co-operate in a plan to fly to an Allied base, all quite absurd, kept us going.

But now – this was it! Barbed wire, with no realistic hope of a rescue plan. How would I survive? What of my health?

A fair bit of my thinking was around myself, my welfare.

At that moment I received my first letter as a prisoner. It was from Mrs General Minnie Carpenter, wife of The Salvation Army's leader. At the end of her letter she added a quote from the Bible regarding Jesus' ministry on earth, 'The Son of Man came not to be ministered unto but to minister.'*

I was forcibly reminded that it would be unworthy to fret and worry about my own condition. My task was to minister and serve others.

*Matthew 20:28

CHAPTER FOURTEEN
Crime and Punishment

TANKY was the type for whom prisoner-of-war life came very hard – one of life's 'losers'. Possessing little emotional and mental reserve, he resorted to stealing from his comrades. He then took the stuff to the barbed-wire where he bartered with an Italian guard.

A prisoner-of-war camp had its own code of ethics. To steal something from your captors was regarded as patriotic but to steal from a fellow-prisoner was the worst possible crime. Therefore, Tanky found himself in 'clink'.

I should explain that after a very brief period of 'mob rule', when the crowd, according to the heat of the moment, administered the punishment it thought appropriate – even to throwing the culprit into an open trench latrine – it was realised that some sort of law and order must prevail. But to administer discipline presented a problem.

How could an offender be punished? To cut a man's food would be impossible; he received barely enough to live on. To confine a man to barracks when no one was ever let out was futile.

The only means of punishment, therefore, was for the offender to be 'sentenced' to so many days in a little barbed-wire enclosure in a corner of the compound. Another piece of wire within wire!

It was the night before Tanky was to come out. The days were rather short at that time of the year. Having no form of lighting, we all turned in at about 5 pm. There we would remain until someone shouted, 'Roll call!' at 8 the following morning. It was impossible to sleep through all those hours so we either talked or just lay thinking.

Tanky belonged to our tent, and the other occupants could hardly be blamed for not being over-keen to welcome back a thief. Except for the voices of the guards shouting to each other every few minutes from their guard boxes, everything was fairly quiet.

Just as I was making another attempt to sleep I became aware of a conversation between two lads who slept further down the tent.

The voices were those of Jock and Rennie. They were talking of the one spending his last night in the 'clink'.

'Tomorrow Tanky comes out,' I heard one of them say. 'What shall we do? It was a rotten thing he did, but Tanky's never had much of a chance in life. He had a very poor home life as a child. Let's go and meet him when he comes out, and say, "Tanky, we want you to come back in our tent and we want to help you to go straight".'

What a gem of a conversation! Two ordinary fellows with no theological training − but they made a profound impression on me as I listened to their conversation in the tent. I was aware of the presence of God because Jock and Rennie experienced the love of God in their hearts.

They had discovered the real secret of a happy life.

CHAPTER FIFTEEN
The Fight from Sheer Boredom

TWO skinny contestants are rising to their feet; there is to be a fight. Word gets round. Two thousand bored men, just waiting for something to happen, converge on the spot.

How time drags in a prisoner-of-war camp! Nothing to do all day. The excitement of being captured has given way to unremitting hours and days of sheer boredom. Once we have swopped yarns about how we were captured, there seems nothing much to talk about because nothing happens. When the occasional bullock cart trundles down the country lane outside the camp we all go to the wire to watch it. At least something is moving.

Dispute

Back to the fight. What is it all about? No one seems interested in what caused it. It is probably a dispute between two men who are in the same group of 'muckers'.

For the purpose of mutual support and survival most prisoners were part of a combine usually numbering between two to six. My 'muckers' were Ray and Harold, with whom I was captured, and Sergeant Paddy Docherty, a colourful character from Londonderry, Northern Ireland. Ostensibly something as simple as an argument as to whose turn it was to wash up the dixie could have sparked off the disagreement – so ridiculous seeing they had all day in which to complete the one-minute task.

The real problem was below the surface: a combination of pressures such as boredom, acute hunger feelings, anxiety about the future, plus the human factor of living in close proximity with mates for 24 hours each day with no personal privacy.

Civilised

As I recall those two emaciated forms coming from their respective corners of the ring, supported by their 'seconds', the event seems so civilised compared with so much violence today. There were strict rules to be observed; you didn't hit below the belt, you never hit a man when he was down, you didn't use your boots and you fought clean.

An assistant Borstal governor recently expressed similar thoughts. 'When I came into the prison service many years ago, if two lads had a grievance against each other they could go down to the gym, put on the boxing-gloves and get rid of their aggression in a civilised manner according to strict rules of "fair play". But those days have gone,' he continued. 'Today it's much more brutal and cowardly. The lights suddenly go out, the boot goes in or a knife flashes. Everyone else disappears leaving the victim in a sad state.'

Frightened

Modern man is also in a sad state. When a man has no longer any respect for God, or others, or himself, he is building a corner in Hell. People become frightened, alienated from God and themselves. The natural outcome is violence.

But, once again, back to the two contestants. This is no 15-round fight – they don't even last one round. No blood flows; there's not even a black eye to remind them of the fight.

Supporters

Urged on by the hundreds of supporters, they momentarily glare at each other, take a couple of steps forward, manage about two hits and then collapse on the ground, exhausted from malnutrition. They haven't enough strength to hurt each other.

They get up, shake hands, and all is forgiven and forgotten!

CHAPTER SIXTEEN
The Great Divide

'THAT'S the "lousy tent",' said Paddy Docherty, pointing in the direction of two unshaven, dejected creatures who were moving around the tent with the air of outcasts.

Sergeant Paddy Docherty of the Medical Corps, who seemed well connected with the camp 'grapevine', explained that the two men had been segregated from the rest of the camp inmates because they were alive with lice – verminous.

They had been isolated, not for their own health and welfare, but to avoid other prisoners becoming contaminated. A social barrier separating the prisoners had arisen.

In pre-war life social divisions existed because of wealth, material possessions, job status or education, creating feelings of superiority or inferiority. But in this prisoner-of-war camp a person was forced to move his place of residence because of a little creature, hardly visible to the eye, and multiplying at an alarming rate, which had taken possession of the seams of his shirt. In this camp the great divide was between the clean and the unclean.

I tried to imagine the feelings of those men as I lay in my tent that night. Not only were they separated from homes and families, and suffering the privations of prison life, but they had also been banished to a spot isolated from their comrades.

To feel rejected is probably one of life's worst experiences. But I also shuddered as I tried to imagine what it must feel like to be unclean, contaminated – lousy.

Segregated

I consoled myself that, unlike so many others, I kept myself clean. I shaved daily and managed to wash regularly, even if I had to line up for an hour to get a turn at the tap, and vigorously apply the piece of pumice stone which served as soap.

On subsequent walks around the perimeter of the camp I noted that more and more tents were joining the segregated group as if they were competing with the birth-rate of the lice. Even more alarming, men from my own little group of tents transferred to the 'lousy' part.

Suddenly life changed dramatically for me. It was Sunday afternoon. The sun shone brightly. The countryside looked picturesque. I was making my way to the camp church service when I had an irresistible desire to scratch.

Horror! 'Surely not!' I thought. I inspected my shirt, and discovered two fat, juicy lice nestling in the seams under the armpit. I had to accept the awful truth: I was as lousy as everyone else! There was no need for a segregation area – we were all in the same condition.

Relentless

The terrible fact was that, despite our daily search and the relentless battle to reduce the number of lice, there was no possibility of complete deliverance.

'I've killed ten,' a voice would proudly exclaim. But for every louse killed a dozen more unseen eggs would be waiting to carry on the relentless war. The clean and dirty were equally contaminated.

With hard work we might reduce the number but never eradicate the condition. We needed an agency outside ourselves, outside the resources of our world. After 18 months in that condition we were introduced to such an agency, a process which dealt once and for all with our condition. I will describe this in a later episode. It was humiliating – but it was worth it to feel free and clean once more.

We all share a common condition of being contaminated in a different way. 'All have sinned and come short of the glory of God,' the Bible says.*

Many people stagger through life never becoming their true selves, the people God intended them to be.

We too need an agency, outside ourselves, to deal radically with our condition, to make us feel clean, and to free us to reach our potential. Christ has died to deliver us from this condition. What a relief when that happens!

*Romans 3:23

CHAPTER SEVENTEEN
Bread Ration

BERT'S smiling face and outstretched hand appearing through the tent flap has become a daily ritual. Bert, of the Corps of Military Police, arrives for his daily ration – not of bread or soup, but of inspiration.

Our most precious possession is handed to him – a little New Testament, picked up two days after we were captured, and shared between Ray, Harold and myself.

As I look now, years later, at that same New Testament, I see many of its pages are loose. Not many New Testaments have been more eagerly read.

Precious

Sometimes it was necessary to say to a man, 'Sorry, it's booked today, but if you come tomorrow we may be able to lend it to you for a short time.' But Bert had a standing order for a daily loan of the New Testament at 4 pm.

Never have I seen men more eager to learn about God. On meeting some of my fellow Christian workers after the war, I sensed that, in spite of the terrible conditions, a part of them longed for those prisoner-of-war days. There had been such a response to the Christian gospel message.

I watch Bert depart with the precious New Testament. He moves away from the tent area to a relatively quiet corner of the compound, close to the barbed wire, to be alone with himself, with the New Testament and with God. He is discovering the truth of the words, 'Man shall not live by bread alone.' Luke 4:4

47

He has known many adventures, yet he is now discovering life's greatest adventure. He is making a pilgrimage into his inner life and finding God.

He is also finding his true self. It seems to Bert that he is tapping resources of power deep within, which he had not previously realised existed. His sense of poise and balance, so necessary when facing the rigours of prisoner-of-war life, is striking.

Bert would explain that there is nothing magic about it. Neither is the Christian adventure all 'plain sailing'. Christian discipleship requires some discipline. Truth to tell, sometimes when he prays and reads the New Testament he is almost barren of feelings; it is necessary then to hold on in faith.

Persistent

The reward for persistent faith will surely come; there will be occasions when time seems to stand still. In the quietness a person can become wonderfully aware of the presence and peace of God. In those moments Bert finds the real purpose of living.

'Thanks,' says Bert, returning the New Testament. 'See you tonight at evening prayers.'

Before retiring to rest each night, Bert joins with a group of fellow prisoners beneath the one dim light near the cookhouse. They commit their lives to the care of God, and pray for fellow prisoners in special need, as well as remembering their families far away.

'Dear Lord,' prayed one lad, 'help us when we're browned off.'

Personal

We were learning that being a Christian was no solitary occupation. The experience gained through personal prayer and Bible reading needed to be tested and shared with others and expressed in caring concern for fellow prisoners.

Years later, as I walked down the shopping centre in Torquay one day, I saw again that happy face which used to appear through the tent flap. Bert told me he looked back with gratitude to God for the enriched quality of life he had experienced in that Italian prisoner-of-war camp.

CHAPTER EIGHTEEN
Too Hungry for Sex

GATHER together a group of servicemen, and it will not be long before at least some of them will begin to exchange dirty jokes and boast about their sexual exploits, real or imaginary.

During the period spent in Italian prisoner-of-war camps, however, I never heard any obscene conversation and was not aware of any homosexual acts amongst prisoners. Later, in the third year of captivity, when transferred to Germany, I was asked to deal with one case of homosexuality – but I will tell about another time.

So what had happened to all those Commonwealth soldiers? Had prison life transformed them into cloistered monks? Was their sexuality being consciously suppressed?

To answer, it will help if we go for a walk around the prison compound and listen in to snatches of conversation between men as they share the thoughts and feelings uppermost in their minds.

We are about to join the company of two men walking around the perimeter with hands in pockets, deep in conversation.

'You get a basin,' says the tall Grenadier Guardsman to his mate from the Durham Light Infantry, 'and you pour in some flour, then break an egg and mix it together, after which you add some grated cheese, and then...' Some men spent their entire existence collecting and swapping recipes which they intended to try out on their return home.

Excited

We move on to another group. They don't consider themselves food fanatics, for they are discussing some of the leave periods they have enjoyed. Nevertheless they soon find themselves trapped by this insatiable hunger.

'There was a marvellous cafe just by the park,' says Terry, his voice sounding excited, and his face wearing an expression of unutterable bliss. 'Fantastic plate of eggs, bacon, sausages and tomatoes!'

The early morning sun is shining through the tent flap when a voice is heard to exclaim, 'Coo, just had a wonderful dream. I was getting stuck into a big plate of meat pie, chips and plenty of gravy. What a dream! Wish it were true!'

You will have guessed why the men were obsessed by thoughts of food. They were very hungry. A bowl of soup and a piece of bread the size of a man's fist was our daily diet. Everyone had the same rations, which meant that the big fellows, over six feet tall, were really starving. I was fortunate in not experiencing the extreme hunger pains suffered by many of my friends.

Prisoner-of-war life taught us that sex was not necessarily the overbearing driving force some experts had claimed. When sex and hunger have to compete, hunger wins easily. In fact, it is hardly a contest because the sex drive in a very hungry person simply ceases to exist.

Sex and hunger are two basic needs, and although hunger is the stronger, they both seem to have one thing in common. When leading a discussion now with a group of boys and young men on the subject of sexuality, I sometimes use the example of the hunger drive to explain how men have to mature and grow up in their understanding of sex.

Primitive

Here is a baby in his high chair at feeding time. Not a

pretty sight. The food is being stuffed into his mouth – sometimes his ears – either with hands or spoon. The food is plastered over his face and some even in his hair and, should you happen to approach, a sticky spoonful will come your way. His hunger is primitive, anti-social. He possesses no social graces. The expression of his hunger instinct is appropriate to his age.

But over the years something happens; a change takes place. One day he takes a friend, maybe a girl-friend, out to a meal. They don't rush straight for the table and get 'stuck in'. They might even say grace. The sharing of a meal has become transformed into a very meaningful occasion resulting in the creation of a relationship or the deepening of a friendship.

It sometimes helps men, as well as adolescent boys, to see that a similar maturation should take place regarding their emerging sexuality. What once was perceived instinct is transformed into a desire to love, to give, to care, combined with a deepening sense of commitment and trust.

We can't do better than seek God's guidance about sex, because he thought of it before we did!

CHAPTER NINETEEN
Parcel Bashing

THE camp was a busy hive of rumours; we lived on them. 'When will the war be over?' was the question continually being asked. According to rumour the Pope visited England about twice a week for peace talks!

Next in popularity to discussion about the war was talk of parcels. Red Cross parcels. Were they, after all, a fairy-tale? It only needed the sound of a train whistle to set off wild speculations about its arrival with the longed-for parcels.

Rumour

I listened for about two hours to two mates having a heated argument as to how they would divide up their parcel between them. Yet they didn't even know what it would contain!

However, the day arrived when the latest rumour was confirmed – the parcels were actually in the camp. Great excitement prevailed and a spirit of goodwill was abroad. 'Why, even if you go to get a wash,' a fellow remarked, 'someone will say, "Can I wash your back, mate?"'

The little Italian colonel, who often appeared unshaven, decided it would be a great day for himself. The atmosphere was like a school prizegiving. The brown cardboard boxes were stacked at one end of the compound, each bearing the names of the British town which had donated it.

Beside a table stood the bemedalled colonel in all his splendour, beaming on us like a benevolent old uncle, with the first parcel in his hands. The rule that prisoners should salute

Italian officers had been rather difficult to enforce. This was to be the colonel's big moment when he was to receive all the salutes possible.

Some distance away we were lined up in fours. The desire for a parcel was stronger than the reluctance to salute. Off we marched to the saluting base, clicked and heels and performed the required ritual. Like Father Christmas himself, the colonel presented us with one parcel between four men. I shared one donated by the people of Southall, Middlesex.

There were two schools of thought regarding the best method of dealing with the contents. The more scientific approach declared that to gain the maximum nourishment from the contents a little should be eaten over a period of several days. Those holding the opposite view were described as the 'parcel bashers'. The food simply disappeared within minutes.

One fellow didn't even bother to put the butter on the biscuits. He spooned the butter, then started on his fourth share of a tin of condensed milk, followed by the corned beef and chocolate. His stomach soon protested painfully against such unaccustomed luxury.

There were those, of course, who wavered between the two views.

Trying to sleep that night was more difficult than usual. Our pillows consisted of our entire worldly possessions. Now the remains of our parcel, if any, shared the honoured place with our boots, beneath our weary heads. Knowing that one's right ear rested on a couple of biscuits, or the fourth part of a tin of corned beef, was not conducive to sleep.

Torment
The silence of the night was suddenly broken by the rustle of paper. Hands shot to pillows. All was well; nothing was stolen. The rustle simply meant someone could no longer

stand the torment. The scientific theory could be ditched – he was 'bashing' his parcel!

Although I couldn't sleep, I lay there and thanked God for such organisations as the Red Cross that undoubtedly saved many lives.

CHAPTER TWENTY
Unfit for Habitation

I SHIVERED as I woke on those November mornings and saw snow on the Appennines and frozen water in the earthenware bowl outside the tent. Hardly an inducement to wash and shave!

I felt that the Italians wanted to help us, but their resources were meagre. Alarmed at the increasing number of men having to be admitted to hospital, they decided to hold a 'thin man's parade'. This meant that those who looked like a human broomstick, with ribs sticking out like a plate rack, stood a chance of getting an extra ration.

Although winter had arrived, many of us were still running around in just the shirt and pair of shorts we wore when captured in the desert. We slept in our clothes at night and during the day we often wrapped our blankets around us.

Indispensable

I should explain that a pack of playing cards was an indispensable part of prison life. For example, each day, when the bread ration came, the cards would be cut, to prevent grabbing and unfairness. Highest card took first pick.

Although I never became initiated into the mystery of card-playing, I picked a card when an assortment of Italian left-off garments arrived for distribution, and became the grateful receiver of an Italian second-hand greatcoat.

Some became the owners of long linen underpants that

tied round the ankles with string. It was comical to see such garments worn beneath a pair of desert shorts, but no one bothered how he looked so long as he kept warm.

A rumour circulated that the Italians were about to confiscate one blanket from each man. To add to the bizarre picture, blankets were immediately transformed into some kind of clothing – scarves, hats, coats, etc. We gave the appearance of a fancy dress parade of men resembling Robinson Crusoe's Man Friday.

Ray commenced a reading circle in the tent, and I gathered a group together before evening prayers for a 'sing-song' in the cookhouse – the only building, apart from the hospital, that had a roof.

Inevitably

Just to make matters worse, it rained and rained. It didn't stop raining for days. Like good boy scouts, we dug a trench around our tents to drain the water away from the walls. But after three days we sat up all night watching the level of water gradually rise in the trench until – inevitably – it flooded the tent.

Next morning, like protest marchers, we each carried one of the small tent poles, about three feet high, and found a piece of higher ground situated between the open ditch latrine and the tents reserved for men with scabies. Our few possessions looked like bundles of soaking rubbish.

As we were wondering how long we could survive in such conditions, members of the Protecting Power from Switzerland – whose task it was, under Geneva Convention, to visit and report on conditions in prisoner-of-war camps – paid us a visit.

It did not take them long to decide that the camp was unfit for human beings and must be closed.

Inspection

As they were making their inspection, one of the representatives casually offered a cigarette to a prisoner. Immediately there was such a dive that the surprised representative was nearly knocked over.

What an awful mental state some of the men were in as a result of craving for a smoke! Some smoked anything – fig leaves, even bits of wood. They would 'flog' their wedding rings or even their meagre bread rations to obtain a cigarette. 'I don't care if I die of hunger,' said one man, 'as long as I die with a fag in my mouth.'

Prisoner-of-war life made me grateful I had never bothered with the weed.

CHAPTER TWENTY-ONE
Passing Out Parade

DRESSED in a motley collection of clothing, a long line of prisoners of war began to form up outside the camp. It had been condemned as unfit for human habitation.

As one of the party to follow later, I watched the main exodus. The men paraded with full kit, which for some consisted merely of a blanket and a small bundle of firewood, in the hope that one day they would receive another Red Cross parcel and be able to boil some water to make tea.

Camp mascot

We knew the past, but what of the future? 'Couldn't be worse than this,' said the guardsman, who had polished his boots for the occasion.

We remembered those who had marched into the camp with us but would not be marching out. Some had died in hospital. Among those attempting to escape was one who had been shot dead while crawling under the barbed wire.

I wondered how much of the emotion of the moment was shared by Timimi, the little three-legged dog who ran after a stone and was patted on the head by the men waiting to move off.

Timimi was the camp mascot. How he came to lose his leg nobody knew. It was thought that he once belonged to a German soldier.

When the British captured a place called Timimi – hence his name – they found the little dog, who soon became attached to his new master. His new master was taken prisoner of war and Timimi shared the captivity. Here he was in Italy, still faithful.

A couple of years later, when we were in Germany, I asked what had happened to Timimi. There was a story that he had wandered into the Russian compound and been eaten by the starving Russian prisoners.

At the front of the march the young piper of the Cameron Highlanders tuned up – or whatever the process of getting red in the face and squeezing the bag is called – 'We'll save you a bed space, Fred,' shouted Harold as he and Ray moved off to the sound of the pipes.

As the piper played them out of the camp I had a feeling of pride. There was almost a sense of occasion. Although thinner than when they had arrived at the camp five months previously, and looking even stranger in their assorted garments, most of them hadn't lost their sense of dignity and self-worth.

The sound of the pipes reminded me that when Tobruk fell – and most of us were Tobruk prisoners – the Cameron Highlanders were the last regiment to give up the fight. When finally they ran out of resources and were forced to surrender, they proudly marched into captivity with the piper at the head.

Prison life was teaching me that everyone has his or her breaking-point. Some can take more than others. A sense of personal worth, self-esteem and inner resources are essential in the preservation of dignity and humanity.

Inner world

For some a new thought began to dawn. Whether or not we are religious, we all have an inner world. What goes on in that inner world will decide whether we live victoriously, survive or disintegrate.

One of the advantages of prisoner-of-war life was that

many people learned more about themselves, including their inner world.

When the sound of the pipes died away I returned to the compound. Now that the hospital was deserted I was able to enjoy the luxury of sleeping in a wooden hut, making a fire and having a light to read by at night.

CHAPTER TWENTY-TWO
Off Guard

LOFTY stroked his ginger beard and grinned. 'This is the life,' he exclaimed as he lay on a camp bed absorbed in Agatha Christie's *Ten Little Nigger Boys*.

But although most of his concentration focused on the unfolding plot, his left hand shot out when Charlie's South African accent announced, 'Tea up!' Thank goodness someone had saved some tea from their Red Cross parcel!

That morning we had said goodbye to our mates who had departed for Camp PG 70. Our numbers had dwindled from 4,000 to four, so we transferred to the now disused camp hospital hut for the few days until we too would depart.

It was amazing how within a few hours the relationship between guards and prisoners changed. When Charlie was struggling to light the fire for the brew of tea, Iaccio, one of the guards, triumphantly produced a piece of wood, a precious commodity in a prison camp. Then, demonstrating his versatility, he detached – after a struggle – the rusty bayonet from his rifle and proceeded to use it as a chopper for firewood.

We immediately warmed towards Iaccio, who in turn visibly relaxed. 'Do you want some tea?' asked Charlie.

Within minutes, four prisoners and two guards were sitting round the fire, rifles and bayonets parked in the corner of the hut.

Party
In the ensuing party atmosphere we sang songs and

entertained each other. Baccante, the second guard, who had been a sailor, entertained us with graphic descriptions of his adventures. But how can an Italian guard with no knowledge of English communicate with English prisoners whose knowledge of Italian is limited to such words as bread, water, food, tomorrow, etc? No trouble at all.

In the space of an hour we learned most of his life story as he pranced about, gesticulating to illustrate various episodes in his life. It went something like this: 'Brrrr, brrrr, brrrr' – the sound of an engine – accompanied by a mime with his hands simulating the action of turning a steering-wheel.

'Got it!' shouted Lofty, as if it were a party game of charades. 'He used to drive a lorry.'

Then came family information. A sudden look of bliss crossed Baccante's face as he pointed to himself and said, 'Woman', one of the few English words he knew.

'He's got a wife,' interrupted Charlie.

'How many children?' asked Lofty, simulating the nursing of a baby.

Baccante held up three fingers. Then followed a mimed version of some of the exotic delights of his foreign travels. All very good fun.

'Not bad, those Eyeties, when you get to know them,' said Lofty when the guards had departed and we were enjoying the luxury of lying in our camp beds before putting out the light. We were warm, a roof protected us from the rain and, as an added bonus, there was electric light.

Until the previous night we had slept in tents – although that is rather an exaggerated description of the structures. Insufficient tent sheets meant that we couldn't make a complete tent. Therefore we were exposed to the wind and weather.

Excursion

It got dark at about 4.30 during December, and as there were no lights anywhere in the camp we couldn't walk around the perimeter. So we were forced to lie down between 4.30 and 8.30 the next morning when someone shouted, 'Roll call!' which saw us clutching our one blanket around us and staggering to the centre of the compound, to line up in columns of five. We were counted by Italian guards not chosen for their mathematical skills.

Like a dramatic scene-change in a play, next morning saw us actually outside the prison camp being taken for a walk by none other than the Italian colonel and one of his sergeants.

A lady stepped out from among a group of wide-eyed villagers, curtsied politely to the colonel and asked permission to offer the British prisoners some wine. The village ladies noticed that my eyes were drawn to the strings of corn cobs draped down the side of some houses, giving the whole wall an orange colour. We chatted, laughed and listened to their English gramophone, with its big horn and the familiar picture of a dog listening to music, playing records – a pleasant reminder of England.

They wished us 'good voyage', and gave us some corn cobs. We thanked them and said goodbye.

Our next stop in the village was at the home of the sergeant. He quickly kindled a fire in the big open fireplace, produced a kind of saucepan with holes in the bottom on which he roasted chestnuts which smelt and tasted delicious.

Our excursion outside the wire had been most cordial and informal right until the moment when, as we entered the camp, I handed the sergeant his rifle which I had been carrying for him. All quite ridiculous but most enjoyable.

CHAPTER TWENTY-THREE
Moving Experience

'SORRY Lofty isn't with us,' said Charlie as we stood waiting for the train at Lucca Station. Reduced to three in number, we were on the way to our next prison camp.

Our last glimpse of Lofty was his long thin figure, topped by beard and a mass of curly hair, perched on an antiquated carriage pulled by a pony. A guard, complete with rifle, was squeezed in at the back. Desert sores on both legs had refused to heal, so Lofty was to be admitted to the town hospital for treatment.

Thoughts about Lofty and musings about our uncertain future were interrupted by the approach of three Italian women. From their shopping bags they produced what was probably their day's bread ration, brought to be eaten with some soup they hoped to obtain in a restaurant at Lucca.

As they handed their bread ration to three unknown hungry prisoners it was like a sacrament. I could recall the words of Jesus – 'For inasmuch as you have done it unto the least of these, you have done it unto me.'

We three prisoners were the last to leave Camp 60, which was condemned as unfit for prisoners.

A short journey of half-an-hour was followed by a five-hour wait on a station platform. Our dirty, unshaven guards directed us to a waiting-room where we became the centre of a crowd of inquisitive onlookers, for whom the presence of prisoners of war was an unusual sight.

There increasing numbers made it necessary for us to be transferred to another room. With such an audience present, the guards were encouraged to show their authority by gesticulating, shouting and ordering us about. We paid little attention.

The fun really started when the train eventually arrived. Everyone rushed for the doors, pushing and struggling like animals. The corporal of the guard rushed from one end of the train to the other, appealing breathlessly to officials for a carriage for his three prisoners. The three other guards were in a similar panic, sending us to one end of the train and then to the other. We finally decided to remain put until they really made up their minds.

The train was about to depart, but we were still on the platform. The corporal, now in an exhausted state, made one last appeal to the station-master, who dived into a carriage already hopelessly crowded. To their annoyance, he ordered everybody out. One man protested so wildly he had to be arrested by the police and, complete with baggage, was carted off to the nearest lock-up.

After we had travelled some hours and halted at many stations, midnight found us at Bologna, the main station in Italy. At four the next morning we reached the final station, Port San Georgia. Few people were about. We went to a waiting-room, stretched ourselves on forms and fell asleep.

Two hours later – it was still dark – we were marched out of the station along a deserted road. After a cup of coffee, costing us one lire, we boarded a tram with a number of fellow travellers who were on their way to work.

First light

In the first light of the morning we were aware of the tram going down a hill. At the bottom we could make out some lights in the form of a square which seemed to come rushing up at us. We immediately identified this as our next prison camp.

Soon we would know our fate. Experience had taught us to hope for the best but prepare for the worst. We approached our new prison with mixed feelings.

'Camp 70', as we called it, had a most prepossessing entrance. We passed under a huge arch with the words 'Camp Concentramento Prisioneri de Guerra' inscribed across the top. 'Look at that!' said Charlie, as we passed through the arch. 'Cultivated flower beds set in a courtyard with imposing buildings.'

After the mud, water, and little tents at Lucca, the permanence of this place looked reassuring. It did not take us long to discover that the flower beds, courtyard and imposing buildings were not for us.

Still, what were the words of St Paul, who himself had been a prisoner in Italy? 'Who shall separate us from the love of Christ? shall tribulation, or distress, or persecution, or famine?... Nay, in all these things we are more than conquerors through him that loved us.'

Romans 8:35, 37, *Authorised Version*

CHAPTER TWENTY-FOUR
Laughter and Sadness

THE huge gates of Camp 70 opened and we were swallowed up with thousands of other prisoners.

Ten months were to pass before I would go through those gates again, and then in circumstances which I would never have imagined or anticipated.

Before the war Camp 70 had been a canning factory. The large buildings could sleep 250 men in three-tier bunks. True to their promise, Ray Davey and Harold Barker had saved me a bed space next to theirs. I was the possessor of a top bunk with its advantages and disadvantages.

As a top bunker I would be spared all the dirt and lice falling from above. But at 'skilly' time on a wet day, owing to a complete absence of space for any tables and chairs, it was necessary for the top bunker to climb up on his perch, carrying his pot of skilly, and remain there to eat it.

While arranging my few possessions under the head of my palliasse, I was bombarded with questions. 'Have you got any war news?'

In touch

Most days I was asked the question, 'When will the war end?' I once heard two men talking at night as they lay in adjoining bunks. 'When do you think the war will end?' one asked. His mate replied, 'About three months.' 'Do you really think so?' 'Well, that's what Fred Hill says, and he's in touch with God!' Some men thought I had a 'hotline' to God!

Ray and Harold filled me in regarding conditions in Camp 70. As it was a new camp the International Red Cross had yet to be notified of its existence; it was likely to be some time before Red Cross parcels started to arrive. The guards were smarter and more disciplined than at Camp 60; two roll calls instead of one were the order of the day.

The roll calls were tedious affairs lasting about three-quarters of an hour. Prisoners paraded in groups of 50. Young prisoners, trained for action, cannot stand for three-quarters of an hour in quiet meditation like monks. To make the parade bearable some read books. There was always an interesting person to talk to, or the comedians amongst us would provide a running commentary.

'The camp gate is now opening and – yes, here he comes, a fine example of Italian manhood!' It is a round-shouldered, spotty-faced lieutenant. Various nicknames were given to the guards, such as 'Scarface', 'The Yank', 'Lightning'.

The lieutenant and corporal arrive at our group. 'Attention!' shouts a voice.

Too much

In theory 50 pairs of heels should smartly click together, but those recently arrived from Benghazi have no boots or only home-made shoes. The nervous corporal's lips are moving as he counts, 5, 10, 15, etc. But the 'micky-taking' proves too much, his embarrassment increases, he loses count – and starts again, to the accompaniment of loud guffaws of laughter.

But suddenly silence falls on the 8,000 men. Slowly before us a comrade's body is carried out. We note the number '9' chalked on the side of the coffin.

Nine have died so far. Within two months in Camp 70 the number will have risen to 40. It will be some time before their next of kin will be informed. What a relief it had been when earlier they had learned their son or husband was, at least, safe in a prisoner-of-war camp! But now...

We thought our conditions bad in Camp 60. But the men recently transferred from the Benghazi desert camp, where they had languished for six months, were far worse. Weakened by dysentery and still wearing their desert kit – shirt and shorts – they looked like phantom figures as they shuffled around the camp.

One told me that in Benghazi, because of their physical and mental deterioration, some would be heard howling like dogs at night.

Here was a great challenge to help restore the health and sanity of these men.

*Fred Hill (right) with his mobile canteen, outside
the Salvation Army's Hostel for Servicemen in Cairo.*

*My driver, Stan Bellringer, on
the lookout for enemy planes,
dive-bombing in the desert.*

*Y.M.C.A. staff relaxing at
Anzac Cove.*

A queue soon forms when the canteen hatch is opened.

With fellow prisoners at Hartmannsdorf. (Fred Hill fourth from right, back row.)

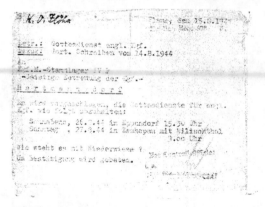

The authority given to my guard when accompanying me on visits to camps.

CHAPTER TWENTY-FIVE
The Disappearing Sentry-box

IT was winter when we arrived at Camp 70. Heating of any description was absent from the Italian camps I knew. Many prisoners were in poor physical condition, and the majority were not anxious to do anything, even attend lectures.

Then gradually a pattern of life began to evolve. Church life was established. Then followed educational classes. After some months an active community had arisen.

Articulate

On some evenings Harold Barker could be seen putting the church choir through its paces in preparation for Sunday. Elsewhere a discussion group would be in progress. An articulate communist, whose views later underwent a great change, would be enthusiastically holding forth.

Little cards, similar to those displayed outside shops at home, could be seen pinned to trees. Instead of the familiar 'Bicycle for sale' or 'Furnished room to let', one would read 'Bundle of firewood for sale – price two cigarettes'. Another card would announce that desert shorts could be made into a forage or peak cap – for two cigarettes.

One enterprising fellow advertised a laundry. I don't think he became one of the camp's capitalists. We already possessed enough lice without picking up more from other prisoners' clothes.

To break one's false teeth need not be cause for worry. One simply had to stroll round to the bunk of a certain quartermaster-sergeant. A row of dentures, some much worse than our own, would be on show. Possessing only a penknife, a nail file and a bolt which he used as a hammer, this quartermaster-sergeant, with no previous experience, would cut up Italian aluminium spoons to make plates and rivets.

After some months, the camp received Red Cross parcels. When the 'makings' of a brew were to hand, the brewing-up pitch was a lively scene.

Inventive

With 8,000 men looking for a few sticks of wood to boil their tea, some inventive skills were called for. For the first few days after parcels arrived, hammering could be heard in the huts as hundreds of men manufactured stoves out of Red Cross tins. With a borrowed home-made knife, a nail and a piece of stone, tins were flattened, then joined together by folds and assembled. From the primitive efforts of the first few days there finally emerged the Rolls-Royce of brewing-up stoves, incorporating a blower similar to a blacksmith's and guaranteed to boil a pint of tea on the tail of an old shirt.

After our first prisoner-of-war Christmas I asked a fellow what kind of Christmas he had had. 'Oh, we had some good brews,' he said, 'but look at my bunk.'

I looked underneath. The bed-boards had disappeared; his palliasse was resting on string. He grinned, 'It was worth it!'

Others were even more adventurous in their search for wood. A guard's attention was diverted to another part of the compound. When he returned his sentry-box had disappeared. Glorious thought – hundreds of lovely brews!

Valuable

'Any embers?' one would shout on approaching the 'brewing-up' patch, home-made stove in hand. 'Here you are,' would come the reply from a lad whose pot was boiling. The valuable embers would be carefully transferred.

'Any embers?' That provided the message for my next Sunday sermon. God had a work for all of us in the camp; it was to hand on to another an ember of faith and hope.

CHAPTER TWENTY-SIX
Motivation to Live

THE sun was sinking below the horizon as the Italians performed the ritual of changing guard. I walked towards the building where about 200 of us slept in three-tier bunks. It was time to turn in.

I had just had a stimulating conversation with Victor, whose eyes lit up with prophetic fire when he talked of how problems of the world could be solved through communism. As we walked around the perimeter Victor, with a piece of army blanket around his neck for a scarf, held forth. 'Crime will diminish. When everyone is given a share, greed and envy will disappear.'

Idealist

Victor was an idealist. I admired him. He had a vision of a future when there would be equality and social justice. 'Of course,' he emphasised, 'anyone thwarting such Utopian plans would be ruthlessly dealt with.' I noted that his philosophy was all about the future and had no message for the present.

Ray Davey, my Irish friend, was also coming towards our building with another prisoner who obviously hadn't shaved for some time. He was a 'bed squatter'. The united Christian church in the camp had become concerned about some men who, helped by the proximity of the bunks, particularly the bottom ones, could remain in them without being observed. They could literally disintegrate and fade away.

Some did just that: simply gave up and drifted out of

this world. The padre had challenged all Christians to walk them around the camp and revive motivation to live. Ray Davey was on such a mission. The Christian anti-bed-squatting group was probably responsible for saving some lives.

About four of the most verminous-looking prisoners were sitting on Harold Barker's bottom bunk when I arrived. A similar number would be there most nights. I used to call them Harold's disciples. Harold would give them a pep talk, make them laugh and inspire them to go on.

It always seemed to me that after such a session they would walk out squaring their shoulders, prepared to face another day. What they never knew, and Harold certainly would not tell them, was that he himself was very ill.

There were some men who might have claimed to be Christians but did not possess the same quality of spirit as Harold.

The bunk groaned as I climbed to the top and tucked my greatcoat around my one blanket. As I slid beneath my blanket and was thanking God for all the blessings of the day, and for the fact that we no longer slept in tents, I became aware of the rugged figure of Patrick standing on a nearby top bunk, facing some of his Irish compatriots.

With a dramatic gesture he bared his large chest. A defiant smile was on his face as he shouted, 'Come on all you Catholics! Come and have a good look at King Billy before you go to sleep!' And there, tattooed on his chest, was a large picture of King William of Orange.

Although it was funny, it was also sad. Such sectarian rivalry can lead to bitterness which has no place in the Christian gospel of God's love, and certainly found no support in the united church within our prison camp.

Fantastic

During the night I was aware of the bunk shaking.

Harold was having one of his malarial bouts.

'You've had a bad night, Harold,' I said next morning.

He ignored my comment. His first words were, 'I have been thinking. There is a fellow in one of the corner bunks who is letting himself go. How can we help him?'

Harold had more reason to pity himself than anyone, yet he never did so. He always thought of others. He lived in the spirit of Jesus who said that if a man tries to save his life he will lose it, but if a man loses it – or, in other words, gives it away in adventurous service to God and others – he will save it.

A fantastic bloke was Harold, a constant example of how a true Christian should live.

CHAPTER TWENTY-SEVEN
Life – And Death

WITH a pile of old tattered books begged from others in the compound, I made my usual morning visit to the prison-camp hospital. As I entered the large, cool building a voice from the first iron-framed camp-bed greeted me with, 'What's the time?'

Further along, another man with a hollow feeling in his stomach asked, 'Got the time?' The same persistent question came from all parts of the lofty room. Why this interest in the time? There were no appointments to keep, no girl-friends to meet.

Eyes periodically roamed towards the door for the sight of two men who would carry in the daily 'skilly' ration. I came across somebody actually working out the minutes to its arrival.

Sadly I noticed one or two patients whose skilly from the previous day was untouched. The poor men were past caring about food. Most probably they were malnutrition cases. Usually they experienced no pain, scarcely seeming to realise their condition. They simply felt terribly tired and weak – and just 'drifted' out. Next morning at roll-call another coffin would be carried out.

'Another has pegged out,' someone would say. Life was casual. I would feel sad that there had been no loved ones near to hear the last words or ease the passing. I felt a great sense of responsibility as I stood before those men each Sunday knowing that for some it might be their last Sunday on earth.

One morning I noticed that there was something different about the hospital patients. What – no talk about food? As I sat on his bed one of them said, with a little more animation than usual, 'It was rotten about the fellow who committed suicide this morning.'

He leaned forward in a confidential manner, and added, 'I feel sorry for his wife and children, but it has been something different to talk about, hasn't it?'

Crises

How strange that such a morbid subject should be welcomed as a new topic of conversation! It broke the awful monotony of life; at least something had happened. Men trained and prepared for warfare found themselves completely lost and unprepared to face emotional and spiritual crises resulting from loneliness and boredom.

To get the men arguing or discussing something other than food was the great need.

Each afternoon I arranged some form of entertainment in the hospital, usually a talk or a lecture. I worked on the assumption that within everyone there is a story waiting to be told. The topics ranged from 'The life of a London bus driver' to 'Workings of the Stock Exchange', or 'Rackets connected with dog racing', and many other subjects.

One young man entitled his talk 'From Borstal to the gallows'. His description of the meals made the prisoners long to be Borstal boys! I was surprised at the way some of the 'ordinary' chaps could lecture on a variety of subjects.

If stuck for a lecturer I could always go to Ginger. With a grin, he would slide down from his top bunk and follow me to the camp hospital. Having spent 15 years in the army he could hold forth with some authority on 'The life and training of a regular soldier'. But when he waxed eloquent on such subjects as Egyptian law, the workings of the War Office and, even more surprisingly, the training of a debutante for court, one wondered where he had picked up all the information.

What a lot of really decent, helpful fellows there were! Most were only too glad to be of service to others.

There were also other kinds. One day I noticed a tall, obviously well-educated member of the Tank Corps. 'Here is a man with something to give,' I thought. But when I approached him about helping the hospital patients he said, 'What do you think I am? A philanthropic society? I don't intend to do anything for nothing.'

After the war I chanced to meet him in Regent Street, London. He seemed like a man with a shrivelled soul; always thinking of himself. How poor he was!

CHAPTER TWENTY-EIGHT
For an Ordinary Bloke

The barrack-room door is dramatically swung open, revealing a breathless figure. He is about to make an announcement. Could it be – the end of the war?

No. 'They're taking the skilly off the fire,' he shouts. Then with excitement like the commentator at the Grand National, he gives running comments on the progress of the skilly pot from the cookhouse – 50 yards away – to where our group of 50 men is impatiently waiting.

I grab my earthenware pot and join the queue. Someone remarks that the pot would look better with an aspidistra stuck in it. Originally we were issued with aluminium dixies, but the urgent needs of war production demanded their replacement by flowerpots. Many of them have already been broken. We stand armed with the only two pieces of eating equipment ever issued to us in Italy – the pot and a spoon.

'It's coming,' someone shouts. Sure enough the two skilly carriers – each holding the end of a pole inserted through the handles in the container – turn the corner. Fifty pairs of eyes focus on the moving objects as if it were the crown jewels coming towards them.

With a dull thud the skilly pot is placed on the ground. Each man will receive the equivalent of one-and-a-half mugs of soup. About seven dessertspoonsful of this will consist of vegetables. Apart from seven ounces of bread and a piece of cheese the size of a matchbox, this will be our only meal for the day.

Once a week small objects identified as meat floating

about in the skilly indicate that the day's cheese ration has been withdrawn. Every six weeks we received a fat ration consisting of one teaspoon of olive oil which was promptly used for hair oil.

Watery soup

Now the great moment has come – the ladling out of the soup. Two operations are involved requiring two implements, first a tin can nailed to the end of a stick to ensure an accurate and fair share of the contents for each man, and secondly a piece of wood with which to stir the soup – otherwise the first in the queue might receive all the vegetables and the last in the queue be left with a mug of watery soup. 'Hi, mate, your hand wobbled,' protests a keen observer who feels sure some of the soup being ladled out missed his pot. Food was number one priority.

Although food was necessary for survival, some men were becoming aware of another kind of hunger, a hunger to discover the real meaning of life.

As Jim Drew was bending an old piece of tin into shape, making a brewing-up stove from empty Red Cross tins, he talked of his past life. He was something of an adventurer. A spell in the Merchant Navy, sheep farming in New Zealand and, for a short time, even a bit of smuggling had added interest and sparkle to his life. Yet he could just as eagerly switch over from bashing a piece of tin into shape to becoming absorbed in a poetry book.

Because he possessed mental reserves and a degree of self-reliance, prisoner-of-war life did not hit him so hard as it did some other fellows. Whenever stuck for someone to give a lecture to the hospital patients, I could always count on Jim Drew helping out with a colourful story from his life.

But he had to become a prisoner to learn the greatest lesson of his life. Suddenly he stopped his tin-bashing, looked up and said, 'I never realised that Christianity was for an ordinary bloke like me. I thought it was just being pious.'

He was one of 82 men who, during a six-day evangelistic campaign in the camp, decided to follow Christ.

Being aware of the spiritual hunger in the camp, my two YMCA friends, the methodist padre, two local preachers and myself prayed and studied together in preparation for the campaign. The main emphasis was on the training of the converts.

The methodist minister, who had collected a bullet in the stomach during the El Alamein battle, drafted out most of the follow-up talks.

After the campaign, the converts were formed into small fellowship groups for instruction on Christian beliefs and living. It was in one of these groups that Jim Drew learned more about the victorious way of living. This adventurer found life's sublime adventure – following Christ.

CHAPTER TWENTY-NINE
Conditions are Improving

IT is now ten months since I arrived at Camp 70. Conditions have begun to improve.

A consignment of British clothing has arrived in the camp and I am the proud wearer of a British battle dress, boots and a side hat. A fellow prisoner has adorned my battle dress with Salvation Army insignia. He took some threads from a towel and embroidered the words, 'Salvation Army', on to pieces of old blanket.

With specially printed prison camp money we can, in theory, purchase some things from a canteen. 'Canteen' is an exaggerated description as all we seem to be able to purchase is onions, nevertheless I understand they are good for one's health and help in the cold winter months.

Discipline is being enforced and a new society is emerging. On parade one day the Regimental Sgt. Major conducting the parade asked a lad to step forward to where he was standing. With hands in his pockets he sauntered forward in a nonchalant manner affecting the air of 'What does discipline matter when we are all prisoners?' With a piercing look and a commanding voice the Sgt. Major ordered, 'Take your hands out of your pockets!' Like a shot out of a gun those hands went smartly to his side as he stood to attention. Without some discipline the prison camp could have deteriorated into anarchy.

With many hours of enforced leisure, those fit enough and sufficiently motivated could improve their knowledge. Teachers were found willing to give their services. As text books were almost non-existent, only teachers who could memorize their subject were any good. Later some books did arrive but for security reasons the hardback covers were torn off in case escape material, such as maps, were secreted within the cardboard. As there were no desks or seats, scholars squatted Indian style around the teacher. Some musical instruments bought from the Italians, plus three piano accordions donated by His Holiness the Pope, saw the beginnings of quite a respectable orchestra.

Budding actors formed a theatre group and produced Dickens' 'Christmas Carol', followed by the musical, 'The Desert Song'.

Gradually the prison camp became alive and on a summer's evening one could stroll around the camp looking at the various activities and interests taking place.

As Red Cross parcels arrived more frequently, clouds of smoke would ascend from the brewing-up patch where men were boiling water to make tea.

Past the long queue outside the barber's tent would be a crowd enjoying an outdoor variety show or a general knowledge quiz. Further along one would admire the agility of members of the tumbling group.

Under one of the trees a newly arrived prisoner is giving a lecture entitled, 'The Tunisian campaign', and nearby another lecture is being given on the subject 'Ten days of freedom', by the latest escapee who had been recaptured and was basking in the glory of one who at least 'had a go'.

The latest edition of Camp 70 Times would be displayed on a wall of one of the buildings. Owing to shortage of paper only one copy could be printed, but with the combined efforts of trained journalists, cartoonists and artists an excellent paper was produced.

Sgt Ken de Souza of the R.A.F. provided much of the inspiration for this venture and was convinced that the publication of the paper would do much to raise the morale of fellow prisoners. But what a contrast with the Ken de Souza who arrived in the camp a few months previous. As a R.A.F. observer his plane had been brought down in North Africa. He and his pilot survived four days in the desert without food or water, being forced to drink urine. His privations affected him physically, and for a time, mentally. My first memory of Ken was of his ghost-like figure shuffling painfully around the compound supported by his pilot companion who literally nursed him back to health. When sufficiently recovered Ken was eager to relieve the sufferings of others. Later he successfully escaped and arrived back in England where he informed the Salvation Army that he had met me. He now lives in Bournemouth.

CHAPTER THIRTY
Prisoner-of-War

AFTER food, the most important subject of conversation was probably news. Once the basic survival instinct of hunger was satisfied, war news became priority number one because it determined how long we would remain prisoners of war.

As 1943 advanced, so the tempo of events speeded up, coming to a head in the autumn. First Tripoli fell, followed by the whole of North Africa. An Allied landing in Italy could bring our release within weeks.

About this time, a staff sergeant of the Engineers managed to rig up a radio set. When the coast was clear he would remove a small panel in the ceiling, where the radio was hidden, climb down on to one of the top bunks and give a summary of the BBC news.

'German planes bombed London last night and two planes were brought down.' Slight pause. 'There is a "dig for victory" campaign in England. Churchill says everyone must use any available garden space to grow such things as potatoes to help the war effort.'

Then, glancing round to ensure everyone is listening – and keeping the best news to the end – he announced, 'And there has been an Allied landing at Reggio Calabria, Italy.'

Thunderous applause greeted this news, until the lookout at the door shouted, 'Eyeties!' As the first Italian guard entered the building, the staff sergeant was saying, 'And that is the end of my talk on football.'

At last the big day was at hand. No longer were our

forces separated from us by sea and desert; they were actually on the same mainland as ourselves and advancing towards us. 'Home in a few weeks' time,' was the thought as we began taking each other's home address.

Soon we learned that Italy had capitulated. On the Sunday of that week I conducted the service in the hospital, preaching on Hebrews 13:13 – 'Let us go therefore unto him without the camp, bearing his reproach.'

After the service I went for my usual walk around the camp perimeter, and noticed a number of men, with bags packed, going over the barbed wire to make their own way south towards the advancing British lines or north to the Swiss border.

By this time the Italians were no longer guarding the perimeter and the amplification system was controlled by the British. Suddenly, over the loudspeakers came the chimes of Big Ben followed by a BBC announcer introducing a church choir from somewhere in England.

The singers had no idea of the joy they were giving to hundreds of prisoners who were, at that moment, thinking of their families, with the prospect of soon sharing the family fireside with them.

Next day prisoners belonging to the Brigade of Guards mounted guard using the Italians' rifles. The eyes of onlooking Italians popped out of their heads as they witnessed the performance of the British Guards – heads erect, arms swinging. The regimental sergeant-major exercised his best parade-ground voice, directing the breathtaking precision drill. They couldn't have done better had they been changing guard at Buckingham Palace.

Like a play in several acts, the situation developed. The next act saw our Italian guards setting out on bicycles, waving goodbye as if they were going for a holiday. But why were they going so suddenly? Were the Germans near? We were informed that the Italians were departing because they had received no pay and their food was bad.

So what should we do? We learned that the Germans were retreating northwards; therefore it would be wise to remain in the neighbourhood and return each night to the camp.

Then followed eight days of glorious freedom. It was heaven to wander around the countryside without being shadowed. The trees were crammed with ripe fruit. Grape vines dangled enticingly. When we tired of the vines, there were always peaches and apples. It was amazing to think that over that quiet countryside 8,500 prisoners were wandering just as we were. The villagers were poor, friendly but a little scared. Each night we returned and weighed up the situation.

Surely the Eighth Army would arrive soon. Even if the Germans thought of moving us they would not have the transport. And if they tried, the RAF would put bridges out of action.

The answer came swiftly and suddenly. One morning, when we were frying eggs and everyone was looking forward to another day's freedom, the bugle blew. The lads 'fell in' to receive further information. Formalities over, the parade was dismissed.

But who was that on guard in one of the sentry-boxes? Was it one of our own men? He wore a long peaked cap covered by camouflaged steel hat and carried a machine gun under his arm. He was followed by another – and another.

We looked at each other. After all the wonderful hopes we'd experienced, the awful truth dawned. We were surrounded and recaptured – by the Germans.

CHAPTER THIRTY-ONE
Mad Dash for Freedom

THE Germans who captured us – for the second time – said they would be leaving in 36 hours. They did – but not before a crack German guards regiment had taken over.

One of our number, out celebrating, returned to the camp a little the worse for drink. On seeing a new uniform at the entrance he threw his arms round the German's neck and said, 'Thank God the Americans have arrived!'

The next few days produced a crop of rumours. One moment hopes would soar, only to be dashed to the ground the next. Each morning we woke to find the Germans still there. The arrival of about 20 railway trucks outside filled us with forebodings.

Explanation

Eager to clutch at any straw of hope, we reminded ourselves that the Germans were raiding the countryside, stealing all livestock – a possible explanation for the trucks.

At 4 pm one Thursday, Compound Number One was told to be ready to move. The worst was really going to happen. Where were we bound for? It might be anywhere in the vast territory under German control. It felt worse than being captured the first time.

Though there were many sad hearts that night, it was surprising how much humour was evident. Men gave vent to their feelings by putting up notices for the arrival of the 8th Army. One read: 'Camp 70 to let. New occupants must be lousy, malnutrition cases and old sweats. Keys and enquiries:

Stalag 252 Germany.' Another message to the 8th Army read: 'We waited for you as long as we could. Now you will find us in Stalag 20 in Germany, and don't be long.'

During the evening, my friend Ray Davey appeared in the barracks looking pale. A German guard drunk with wine had fired a machine-gun burst through the Methodist minister's tent, narrowly missing Ray.

Darkness

In the night many men made their escape. The Germans were understaffed and all the camp searchlights had been put out of action by the prisoners. When darkness came the Germans would fire off flares over the camp and rattle off a few rounds of machine-gun fire. However, this did not deter those who had planned to escape.

Hiding behind barrack-room walls, a whole crowd would be waiting to make a bid for freedom. The next flare would go up. They held their breath and gripped their kit. The flare hung in the air, and then died out. Immediately there followed a mad dash for the wire or the wall. It was just too bad for anyone caught with one leg over the wall or crawling under the wire when the next flare went up.

Others found more ingenious methods of escape. Several members of the dramatic society had played female parts. They managed to find entry into the administrative block and, in full costume, minced their way past unsuspecting guards.

Three years ago I received a letter from one of those escapees. 'Dear Sir, During the war I was taken prisoner of war at El Daba, Egypt, and from thence by road to Tripoli and onwards to Camp 70 in Italy.

At Benghazi I remember seeing a young guardsmanlike chap who was a Salvation Army lad. The story was that he had refused the Italian offer of repatriation as a non combatant, and had elected to stay with his 'flock'.

This man again appeared at Camp 70 at Monte Urano in Italy, and I have been told by Ken de Souza, who escaped 19 days after I did, that you are the same man.

Sir, I would like to thank you for your presence amongst our mostly unwashed masses. You were so calm, and over the years I have wondered about that Salvation Army boy who gave me – and I bet many more prisoners of war – an anchor of hope to cling to.

With sincere thanks for having known, for a short while, a real man, who put his faith and his chosen work before repatriation and a soft spot at home.

It was a privilege to have known you. God bless you and the Salvation Army.

Sincerely, Eric R. Moss, ex.R.A.F.'

The day of departure arrived. The longed-for British advance had proved a forlorn hope. Early that Sunday morning I bathed well beneath a cold tap, knowing enough of prisoner-of-war life to be sure it would be a long time before my next wash. My few belongings I put into a kit-bag I had made out of an Italian tent.

I attended morning service, had my last walk round the compound, where I had exercised for 10 months, and went to say goodbye to the hospital patients.

The big gates through which I had entered 10 months previously, opened, and I went out – not to freedom, but to further captivity.

Charles Symonds escaped from Camp 70 during this period. On his arrival back in England he wrote the following letter to the Salvation Army.

19th July, 1944.

Dear Sir,

With reference to one of your Officers in the prisoner of war camp in Italy (Camp 70) I would just like to let you have my appreciation of the very good work he is doing in the camp.

I managed to escape from the camp two days before the collapse of Italy, and made up my mind that as soon as possible I would notify someone of the good work being done by your Officer.

His name I am sorry to say has slipped my memory but he was a young man with fair hair, and wore glasses and was the only Officer of yours in Camp 70 having been taken prisoner in Tobruck June 21st 1942, so you may be able to place him.

He is fit and well and doing everything possible to keep the spirit of the camp at a high level and is carrying on with his head high and a cheery word and smile for everyone.

May I be permitted to congratulate you and your organisation for training such a man, believe me he is certainly a great credit to you, and I wish him and the organisation behind him all the best wishes from the bottom of my heart for without his assistance and smiles hundreds of men would be despairing.

Hoping that you can trace him in your records and can convey my best wishes and thanks to him.

Yours sincerely,
Charles Symonds,
(LATE) DRIVER R.A.S.C.

CHAPTER THIRTY-TWO
Too Many Bodies and not Enough Room

CLUTCHING the kitbag, I waited my turn to climb into a railway truck outside Prison Camp 70 in Italy.

I thought of my parents at home and hoped for an early reunion. But I was looking at a snake-like train which was to swallow me and disgorge me five days later at goodness knows where.

Protested

On the truck was written in French '40 men or 8 horses'. 'We've already got 40 men in here,' protested a prisoner near the door. But the German guard and his gun won the argument, and we nine were added to the truck.

The good news was that there was enough Red Cross food to give each man a parcel. In the truck we found a dixie can of cold coffee. We were informed that as sanitary arrangements were non-existent the dixie could be used for other purposes.

A shrill blast from the engine, the clanging of truck doors and the sudden movement of the train told us we were on our way. For the next five days this truck would be our home.

Daytime conditions were not too bad. We sat on bags or blanket rolls, though we got tired of having nothing to lean against. The sides of the truck had been occupied before we boarded.

One lad took the lid off a golden-coloured tin and, smiling just as if it were a social event, he said, 'Want a bit of delousing powder?'

'Thanks a lot,' I replied, dipping my fingers into the powder and applying it to the inside seams of my shirt. It couldn't eliminate the lice, but it drastically reduced their numbers.

At night conditions were much worse. Forty-nine men could not lie down in such cramped conditions. A determined effort was rewarded by possibly one shoulder resting on the floor. One was afraid to stretch or alter position, even for a moment. Such folly would bring an incoming tide of limbs to fill the vacated space.

As the twilight filtered through the barbed-wire aperture I saw Harold Barker still sitting upright on his kit.

'I say, Buddy,' he was saying, 'if you put your legs round this way, Ray can rest his head on you. And what about Paddy? Can you find a space to put your head down?'

'But what about yourself?' I asked.

'I'm tip-top,' he replied – one of his favourite expressions. What an amazing fellow, always thinking of others, never himself!

In five days and nights, we were allowed out of the truck only twice to go to the toilet. On the first occasion the German guards had a great surprise.

In the hasty exodus from Camp 70 the few German guards could not search every prisoner, so many clandestine objects found their way into the truck. Men in the next truck to ours soon set to work with saws, hammers and chisels until they had made a hole to freedom – much easier than digging tunnels in the compound.

Escaped

At the very next convenient halting-place, each man

dropped quietly to the sleepers and escaped. Many arrived back in England after travelling via Switzerland.

Flight-Sergeant Ken de Souza chose another means of escape. After removing the barbed wire, he squeezed his body though the aperture at eye level.

Ken and Norman – both airmen shot down in the desert – had planned to escape together. But the plan seemed to go wrong. Instead of waiting until the train slowed down as planned, Ken's body disappeared when the train was travelling fast, and he had left his kit behind. Norman, who had nursed Ken to health after their ordeal in the desert, was very worried. Had Ken slipped and fallen? Was he lying injured?

Despite Norman's fears, Ken arrived safely back in England.

At least we were seeing a bit more of the world. In Austria I was struck by the clean stations, but the people's faces seemed grim. 'We appear happier than they do,' said a Geordie voice, 'and, goodness knows, we haven't much reason to be!'

At that moment the 49 men, with shaky prospects and no water, began singing, 'There'll always be an England'. I think we laughed as much then as at any time during our captivity.

'Look, there are our Italian guards from Camp 70,' said one man, peering at the train travelling alongside. By the strangest of coincidences, our former guards were now also prisoners of the Germans.

At last we stopped at a small station called Jacobstahl. The doors were opened and the guards shouted 'Raus!' and 'Aussteigen!' We presumed it meant 'get out', and we obeyed.

The countryside was flat, bleak and creepy. About a mile away the sombre picture of a group of huts, surrounded by barbed wire told its own story. So this was it! And we had thought not so long before that we were very near freedom.

CHAPTER THIRTY-THREE
The Death Pit

AS the sun began to set on that October evening a shiver came over me. It wasn't so much the cold, but the place seemed eerie.

We had been ordered out of the railway truck where we had spent the last five days and were marching towards our new prison camp. Not a pretty sight - barbed wire, at each corner a sentry-box about 30 feet from the ground, guards sweeping the area with searchlights and the barking of Alsatian dogs. The dogs seemed harmless enough, and probably the guards were only wanting to make an impression, but it all added to the grim picture of Jacobstahl.

Suddenly a weird sound started up. Through the barbed wire we could see the inmates, emaciated and poorly-clad Russian prisoners, doing their best to give us a welcome. Three prisoners were 'playing us in' with battered cornet, trombone and drum.

Touched

We felt deeply touched. But a German officer near us seized a rifle and roared at them as they fled for their lives.

Jacobstahl – 'Stall of Jacob' – was a concentration camp. All the buildings and fittings looked old and rusted, and obviously had existed long before the war. It seemed to house Russians and Jews. One story said it originally accommodated mentally subnormal Germans transferred from other institutions in an attempt to prevent the pure German race from being contaminated by interior stock.

Our first unfavourable impression of the camp lasted all six weeks of our stay.

By the time the guards ordered a crowd of us into a long, low building, the last glimmer of daylight had disappeared. 'Thank goodness we have a roof over our heads,' said Harold, as he recalled unpleasant months spent as tent dwellers. We had caught sight of tents, but the Germans had reserved these for the Italians, whom they now held as prisoners.

Harold – always very practical – triumphantly appeared carrying a 'brew'. He had queued for half an hour to get water, and used a part of a bed-board to light a fire.

Agitated

We were housed in long, low, windowless huts, devoid of light or furniture except for a stove at each end. We were given planks of wood to make shelves three tiers high and stretching the length of the hut. These were our sleeping places. In the darkness friends shouted to friends. An explosion of colourful language indicated that someone was objecting to a bed-board clouting his head.

'I'm over here!' I heard Ray shout, so I carried a plank towards his Irish voice.

Soon everyone slept – our best sleep since we had entered the railway trucks five days before.

'Get outside!' someone bawled, and early next morning found us parading for our first German roll-call. The face of the German lieutenant showed that a crowd of British prisoners produced no soothing effect upon his nerves.

Because of his small stature, peaked cap and knee-breeches, the lads immediately nicknamed him 'Harry Wragg' after the jockey. He had a high-pitched voice, was constantly agitated, and, of course, the British prisoners always laughed at the wrong time.

Some of the men, tired of standing, leant against the wire. Harry Wragg came roaring along, screaming something nobody understood. As no one made a move he brandished his revolver until the top of the magazine fell to the ground. There was a roar of laughter. As punishment, Harry Wragg left us for a few hours still on parade. But most men thought it was worth it.

We were allowed no contact with other compounds. Much about the camp remains inexplicable to me even now. Imagine our surprise when about 12 new prisoners arrived in the next compound, including a well-dressed woman wearing high-heeled shoes and a fur coat!

Most of the inmates seemed to arrive at the camp sick and unable to work. Perhaps Jacobstahl was a 'transit camp' between this world and the next, as most were too far gone when they arrived.

Horrified

Once I visited the camp hospital at the other end of the camp. While returning I was horrified to see a dead body in the corner of a compound. The rest of the poor, wretched inmates appeared quite indifferent. It was a common enough sight to them.

A fellow prisoner told me that during that afternoon he had sat looking across at the Russian compound and had counted 12 bodies being taken into a small hut on stretchers which emerged empty at the other end. Apparently the hut contained a huge lime pit, into which the bodies were tipped without any ceremony. According to Russian and English doctors we were to meet later, 70,000 died in one year.

I felt a deep sense of sorrow for the Russians – some just walking skeletons – as they waited for death. They watched their comrades die, and knew that at any time they would follow. I realised that I didn't know what hardship was.

I recalled the suffering of Jesus on the Cross. I believe that God, through Christ, will remain close to us in the most tragic experiences. Ultimately tragedy will be turned into triumph for Christ's love follows us into eternity.

CHAPTER THIRTY-FOUR
Emotion had Died

THERE were no Red Cross parcels in Jacobstahl camp. We were back on basic rations. Our one meal a day came at about 12 o'clock – soup and potatoes. Germans rations were better than Italian; the potatoes, plus occasional margarine, sugar and jam – all unknown in Italy – helped greatly.

There was no comparison between the treatment we received and that meted out to the Russian prisoners. They received less food and had no blankets. It seemed that they were regarded as expendable, to be worked until they dropped. Sometimes a dead body was concealed for a few days in order to draw his food ration.

British prisoners of war were covered by the Geneva Convention, and the Red Cross made occasional inspections. It was after such a visit that our first camp in Italy was condemned as unfit. Because of the Convention, deaths of prisoners had to be registered, mail was arranged, and Red Cross parcels were sent through the International Red Cross.

No such convention operated between Germany and Russia. Russian prisoners were forgotten men, with no contact from home. It would be no good their appealing to the Germans for better treatment, as they would be ignored.

The British prisoners were more vocal and made representation to the Germans for better treatment. But they were put off with promises of 'Muhlberg', and how wonderful things would be when we got there. We lived for that day with cautious expectation.

However, the day arrived when I took one last look at

Jacobstahl camp. The phantom-like figures of the Russians and Jews, despair written on their features, watched us go. It seemed that for some of them emotion of any kind had died. They just existed.

Our future was bright compared with theirs. Unless the war ended quickly, they had little prospect of seeing home again.

Twenty-five years later a letter from the British Foreign Office dropped through my letter-box. It read, 'I am pleased to inform you that a grant of £275 5s 0d has been approved for compensation for persecution by the Nazis of yourself.'

The German Federal Government had decided to give £1 million to be shared among British people who had been 'persecuted by the Nazis'. My six-week stay at Jacobstahl qualified me for a share. I think we celebrated by buying fish and chips.

Guards

We marched the 11 miles to Stalag 4B at Muhlberg. On the way a potato field proved too strong a temptation. Pockets were quickly loaded before the intervention of the guards!

In Italy the movement of prisoners had caused interest among the local people. Germans, on the other hand, did not look twice at the all-too-frequent sight.

The march would have been easier had we had something in which to carry our kit. Ray Davey carried a blanket full of books. Another prisoner made a valiant effort to hold on to an office typewriter he had purloined in Italy.

We arrived at Stalag 4B at evening and were housed in yellow huts, smelling strongly of disinfectant. It was described as the transit compound, where we spent four uncomfortable nights before being disinfected, deloused and registered.

We were grossly overcrowded – 200 in a small hut – all sleeping on the floor, with no lights. The return journey from the latrine at night was hazardous. Ray summed it up: 'It demanded an acute memory, dextrous navigation, the balance of a ballet dancer and the tact of a diplomat!' As one enraged sleeper said when I trod on him, 'If you walk on my face, you might lift your feet now and again!'

While waiting to be deloused and registered, we learned that there were about 40,000 in the camp. In addition to Commonwealth troops there were French, Poles, Russians, Serbs, Dutch, Belgians and Italians.

Despite the hardship, the previous 18 months had had their fulfilment. I wondered what would happen next.

CHAPTER THIRTY-FIVE
Stripped, Purged, Scoured

IT was midnight when the Germans decided to delouse us. Every prisoner transferred from Italy was lousy. Not even the delousing powder sent out from England could cure our condition. We began to accept it as inevitable.

'How many have you caught today?' was the question we asked each other as we took off our shirts and searched for vermin. Even if we killed every louse, reinforcements would rise up from their eggs.

Like sheep we were herded into the cleansing pen. Powerful lights illuminated three sheep-shearing machines operated by Russian prisoners. The process took less time than it takes to describe it.

Clippers

A weary German guard motioned me to a stool. I sat down as a Russian approached me with the clippers. For a moment fantasy took over; I was back in a London hairdressers. 'How would you like your hair, sir?'

Back to reality, not a word was spoken. The clippers said it all. The first swoop over my head left the impression of a well-worn path across a cornfield. By the third swoop I was as bald as when I made my first appearance into this world.

'You do look funny,' said Ray, laughing fit to burst. My laugh came when Harold and Ray took their turns. If we didn't look like prisoners before, we certainly did afterwards.

We were directed to a room and ordered to strip and

place our clothes and kit in a large cage pulled out of the wall. After it was full I was ordered to help push the cage back into a chamber where it was gassed.

The next operation was bathing, with a battery of showers pouring down on us. In single file we proceeded to another room. At the door sat a Russian prisoner holding a pole, at the end of which was what looked like a wallpaper brush. As we raised our arms disinfectant was applied to our armpits and between our legs. Five minutes later we felt most uncomfortable. That disinfectant was powerful stuff – did it sting!

Next an Italian prisoner dabbed a damp pad on my chest and arm, another stuck a syringe in my chest, and a third grabbed my arm and vaccinated me – all very efficient.

Still in the nude, we lined up in fives awaiting the processing of our clothes in the gas chamber. We talked together until a German sergeant came shouting and raving. It dawned on us that he was trying to tell us to be silent. One prisoner slow to obey was made to stand in a corner like a naughty schoolboy. Somehow, with no clothes on one feels more vulnerable.

At about 1 am the gas chamber was opened and each man searched for his clothes. 'Hi, mate, have you seen my other boot?' someone asked, dressed in his cap and one boot.

When we had finally retrieved our kit, the next stage was the dreaded search. Would they find the Salvation Army money that I had carefully hidden? I sighed thankfully when I lost only my groundsheet in that search.

Despite the humiliating process, it was wonderful to feel clean and free from lice. Never again as prisoners of war were we ever verminous.

Cameras

To complete the cleansing and registration process I sat

looking into a camera. With every whisker of hair gone from my head, I held a slate with the number '261052' chalked on it. The camera clicked, and that was the end of 'cleansing and registration'. I left the hut holding a metal identification disc. I was 'prisoner 261052' and had to wear that disc at all times.

CHAPTER THIRTY-SIX
Camp of Contrasts

PERCHED on a three-tier bunk I sorted out my kit, contrasting life now with that in Italy. Happily there was no need to scratch; we were now free from vermin.

Men were putting home-made coal balls on the stove – the first heating we had experienced as prisoners-of-war.

We still had only one meal a day, but the quantity was increased from eight pounds a week in Italy to 22 pounds in Germany. There were still no tables or chairs, but later some men made tables from Red Cross packing-cases.

Some prisoners who had been in other German camps said Stalag IVB was the worst. We who had been in Italian camps thought it was the best.

Timimi, the three-legged dog brought from Italy, turned up with a litter of puppies. Unfortunately she strayed into the Russian compound and was eaten.

Stalag IVB, Muhlberg, was about half a mile square and accommodated 40,000 to 50,000 men. In contrast to the Jacobstahl camp we were allowed access to other compounds. The Russians were definitely the worst off.

Pitiful

Before leaving Italy we had been given new battledress via the Red Cross. The Russians, however, were a pitiful sight, in all kinds of odd clothing, rags wrapped round their feet and most in clogs. Some, with limbs missing, hobbled on crutches, and one was in a contraption propelled with his hands. He had lost both legs.

Nazi propaganda called them 'Ur-menschen' – primitive men – with no culture, religion or intelligence.

They included a variety of nationalities and features. The White Russian with fair hair and bright eyes, the black-haired Slav with pointed features, and the slant-eyed Mongolian were the most common. They possessed remarkable endurance and comradeship.

Beaten

Russians were often beaten by the guards. But if this happened to a British prisoner there would be an immediate complaint. Sometimes Russians searched our rubbish bins, but they would be beaten if caught by the guards.

The Russians got the worst jobs. They had to empty all the latrines by hand, using a cart drawn by a cow and horse.

At mealtime some of the Russians would stand outside our hut waiting for potato peelings. Once, armed with a bucket, I went to where they stood, dropped the bucket and ran. They made a dive, spilling the contents in the mud. Peelings and mud were grabbed and stuffed into their mouths.

Unlike the British, the Russians received no food or clothes from their own country. They were despised by the Germans, and rejected by their own country for being taken prisoner instead of fighting until they died.

When the day of release came, the British were conveyed home by lorries and aircraft. The Russians were ordered to line up on the first stage of a long march back to their homeland.

The atmosphere in the RAF compound was different from ours. Most of the Army prisoners were North African veterans with 18 months' experience as prisoners. The RAF were comparatively new. One night they were in a comfortable bed in England; the next – having been shot down – they were sharing the austerity of Stalag IVB.

Any new RAF prisoner would be the focus of attention. 'What's the latest war news?' 'What's it like in England?' 'When will the war be over?'

Saluting was often a bone of contention. Put a peaked cap on a mop and a German would salute it! The guards loved saluting and collecting salutes. In the British Army only officers are saluted, but in the German army even corporals were saluted by inferior ranks.

Salutes

Perhaps the attitude to saluting revealed different culture patterns. For example, two recently captured RAF airmen were sauntering, hands in pockets, between the compounds. The German camp sergeant-major was expecting to receive two smart salutes from them. But no salutes were forthcoming.

For the offence the airmen spent the next days in 'clink' where they could muse on the cultural differences. They hadn't tried to be arrogant or awkward, but they were not prepared for the German's expectation of being saluted.

Who was right? Both had expectations which were valid for them.

CHAPTER THIRTY-SEVEN
Christmas in Stalag 4B

I PAUSE, I listen – the sound of hammering. It can't be the latest attempt to dig a tunnel. Tunnellers wouldn't create such a din and draw attention to themselves. It comes from the barracks.

Then it occurs to me – 'We will soon spend our second Christmas in the "bag".'

Last year we raised our mugs of Red Cross tea in our Italian prison camp and said optimistically, 'Next Christmas we'll be back home.' Now, a year later, we were approaching our second Christmas in captivity. What we didn't know then was that it wouldn't be the last.

I entered the barrack room.

'Tin bashers' were at work on improvised tables. Empty tins from Red Cross parcels were being flattened with pieces of stone and passed to another group who cut them into shapes such as stars, moons and angels to decorate the windows. Coloured wrappers from the tins were removed and made into paper-chains.

But what is Christmas without a Christmas tree? This presented us with a problem – but not for long. Where there's a will...! The wood fatigue party who worked outside the barbed wire soon returned triumphantly with a Christmas tree.

'We kind of found it,' they said with broad grins.

How could we decorate the tree? 'A bit of tinsel would look good,' suggested Harold.

Tinsel

Hey presto! – thin strips of tin foil came fluttering down from the sky. The mysterious sight brought men rushing from their huts to collect this ready-made Christmas decoration. Our Christmas tree really did look beautiful.

Where did the tin foil come from? It just happened that the RAF were making one of their nocturnal flights over the area. In order to deflect beams of the German radar system they had jettisoned quantities of tin foil strips.

The sight of the ragged, starving Russian prisoners moved the British prisoners, who decided on Christmas eve to donate some of their own meagre rations to people worse off than themselves.

With many hours to think about the real purpose of life, prisoners were ready to consider the spiritual dimension. So on Christmas eve most of the men went to the RAF compound to sing carols and listen to Harold Barker preach about the coming of God's great gift to this world.

Decorations

The Christmas committee had the day organised, commencing with tea in bed. The barracks was ablaze with coloured decorations. I popped into one of the French huts, but in contrast there were no decorations to be seen.

After a fancy hat competition, there was a cake competition – the cakes being made from bread crumbs. Following a Zulu dance by the South Africans, 'Father Christmas' was carried into the hut in a Red Cross container by four men dressed as fairies, their qualification for such a role being that they had the biggest feet.

Blessing

By courtesy of the 'bottom bunkers', we 'top bunkers' were able to eat our Christmas meal sitting down. We had all saved some food specially for the occasion, and the timely appearance of a Red Cross parcel was an added blessing.

Speeches followed, and I was asked to pay tribute to the wonderful work of the International Red Cross. I had a special reason to be thankful for the Red Cross. Although the German soldier who originally captured me in Tobruk allowed me to take my piano accordion, it was later confiscated by the Italians. Now, as we celebrated Christmas, I was able to accompany the carol singing on a new accordion sent out from England by the Red Cross.

But, like the icing on a Christmas cake, there was one more pleasure to experience. In walked an RAF airman, just arrived in camp. German anti-aircraft guns had forced him to bail out of his plane. Learning that I was in the camp he made straight for my hut, and introduced himself as Ralph Brown, a salvationist from England.

We soon discovered that we had many mutual friends back in England. There was much to talk about and photos to exchange. We also discussed how our Christian faith could help us live balanced, healthy and sane lives as prisoners of war.

Suddenly Ralph looked at his watch. 'It's 1 am. I must be getting back to the RAF compound.'

Time had flown, but Christmas in Stalag 4B had been a happy occasion.

CHAPTER THIRTY-EIGHT
Into the Unknown

RAY DAVEY blew on his hands and stamped his feet. 'You needn't bother,' he quipped, as the guard shoved a cartridge up the spout of his rifle. Surveying the thick blanket of snow outside the camp entrance, Ray grinned, 'It's too cold to think of escaping in this weather.'

He and I were both escorted to the camp commandant's office about half a mile from the camp. As there were 12 chaplains in Stalag 4B, we had both applied to be sent to camps where there was no chaplain.

Several times Ray and I had discussed our feelings about such a move. We were reluctant to lose our friends. Some we had known even before our captivity.

We knew that to say goodbye to Harold Barker would be a wrench. He was older than us, a giant of a character, courageous, self-sacrificing, with great powers of leadership. I agreed with Ray that we sometimes held back to let Harold take the lead when we should have shown more initiative.

The thought filling us with apprehension was, simply, the unknown. The present we knew, the future in another camp might be worse. It could be a case of 'Out of the frying-pan into the fire'.

'Heil Hitler!' said our guard, with a Nazi salute, as we were ushered into the presence of the camp commandant. 'Heil Hitler,' responded the commandant, an amiable little officer who eyed us up and down in a friendly sort of way.

Looking up, the officer said, 'Captain Hill!' I stood to attention.

'Ah! Heilsarmee,' – 'Salvation Army' in German – then with a twinkle in his eye he exclaimed, 'Hallelujah!' He said that our application would be considered. We thanked him, clicked our heels and left the office.

Skilly

As the gate of our prison camp swung open to readmit us, Ray mused, 'I wonder if we shall hear any more about our request?'

Things moved faster than we anticipated. In a few days I learned that I had been appointed chaplain to Stalag 4F based at Hartmannsdorf in Saxony, and Ray was to be chaplain of Stalag 4A based at Dresden.

As I climbed down from my top bunk to collect my evening bowl of skilly for the last time, I was aware of strangely mixed emotions. In two hours' time I would be saying goodbye to all my friends.

I had discovered as a prisoner of war that with friends and a sense of belonging you can face almost any situation. In contrast, friendless and without hope, some men just turned their faces to the wall, gave up and died.

I had been fortunate to have the friendship of Harold, Ray and others, people who had an unselfish desire to help, sometimes at a cost to themselves.

One such was Bill Ray, a natural comic.

One bleak January morning a group of men were standing outside the barracks, roaring with laughter at Bill who was sitting in the middle of an icy puddle splashing about and telling jokes. His only reward for such discomfiture was the smiles on the faces of his fellow-prisoners.

Harold appeared triumphantly with a steaming container and we had our last cup of tea together. Eric Hurst, the editor of the camp newspaper, climbed up on a makeshift table and addressed the men. Speaking on behalf of them he thanked me for what I had done for the men, to which I replied.

Then came the moment to say goodbye. It was 10 pm. I had to carry my kit to a transit compound and spend the night with Italian prisoners before my departure at 3 am. I felt in my jacket pocket. Yes, I had the notebook with the home addresses I had just collected from my friends.

Storm

As I gripped the hands of Ray and Harold I was full of gratitude to those two Christian men for whom life had a great sense of adventure, fun and purpose.

A storm was raging as I turned the barrack room door handle and heard the voice of Harold shouting, 'Take care, see you in London soon, Fred!' Would I ever see him again?

Forward I went, into the storm, into the unknown. Two quotes came to me: 'The future I can face, now that I have proved the past.' ... 'I cannot know the future, but the future is in God's hands and that is better than knowing it myself.'

CHAPTER THIRTY-NINE
My New Home – The Laundry

'COME! Come!' shouted an impatient voice. I opened my eyes. A German guard stood beside my bunk pointing to his watch.

Three o'clock in the morning. I was on my way to Stalag 4F. I jumped into my trousers, gathered my belongings into a kit bag and followed the guard to the search hut. To my relief the search was cursory. Three Russians who were to travel too were not searched. They possessed only their day's ration of bread and sausage meat.

Half-an-hour's walk in pitch darkness and pouring rain found us at a railway station. The guard was friendly and kept up a constant conversation, although I understood very little.

'How long do you think the war will last?' he asked. 'Germany and England shouldn't be at war,' he added.

When we changed trains at Chemnitz I noticed that the platforms were being swept by poorly-clad Russian women prisoners. Everywhere one was aware of prisoners. While waiting for our train, a group of civilians handcuffed in pairs came marching along the platform. Germany seemed to be a country of prisoners.

The door into the little courtyard opened. 'Heil Hitler!' said my guard. The keeper of the door thrust out his hand for the required papers. I had arrived at the headquarters of Stalag 4F, my home for the next 16 months.

Festooned
From the courtyard measuring about 20 square yards I

looked up at the five-storey building, with windows festooned with barbed wire. Before the war it had been a laundry. To have seen bundles of dirty linen arrive and leave beautifully clean must have been a much more satisfying occupation than to observe the comings and goings of consignments of humanity in various stages of hope and, more often, of despair.

This was the headquarters of Stalag 4F.

I was eager to enter the building and learn my fate. As I followed the guard up the stairs to the fifth floor I was aware of a cocktail of smells. A strong smell of garlic. 'That's the French room,' indicated my guard, holding his nose. Then an oily aroma from the Russian room.

Surveyed

'Not too bad,' I thought, when I surveyed the room at the top of the building. I had exchanged a camp of 40,000 men for one housing no more than 200, of whom 16 were British or Commonwealth.

For the past two years, eating had been performed either standing up, sitting on the floor, or perched on top of a three-tier bunk. By prisoner-of-war standards here was luxury, for, in addition to bunks sufficient for 20 men, there were two forms and a long table.

I went to the window and peered down at the village below. I wondered how many hours and days I should spend looking at the stream by the side of the road, and watching German housewives industriously knitting as they queued outside the butchers for their meagre meat rations.

Khaki-clad figures caught my eye as they turned the corner into the courtyard. 'They must be my room-mates,' I thought. Soon the door burst open, and I was in the midst of a crowd anxious to give me all the 'gen' on the prison camp.

Fritz, their guard, marched them each day to a warehouse

where, as members of the headquarters staff, they handled British Red Cross parcels to be despatched to British prisoner-of-war working camps.

In due course I learned the guards' nicknames, such as 'Titch', 'Two-fingered Dick' and 'The Nutcracker', so named because of the peculiar shape of his jaw.

There was fun and friendly banter between these 16 men. Conversation would continue beyond 'lights out' as we lay in our bunks.

Wondered

Eggy – so named because of his bald head – shouts, 'Steve, tell us how you were captured with your boots off.'

'Well, at least I do tell the truth about how I was captured, which is more than some of you do!'

Then Steve dramatically describes how he was asleep in his tent in North Africa when a German rifle appeared through the tent flap, and a voice said, 'Come!' Without any heroics Steve became a prisoner-of-war in bare feet.

'But where do I fit in? What is my job?' I wondered as I went to sleep.

CHAPTER FORTY
Permission to Visit

'STAND to attention!' The colonel glared at me across his desk.

I had heard that he was an explosive character so was prepared for this reception. Obviously he did not regard me as God's gift to Stalag 4F.

I requested permission to visit the 80 British working camps in his area to conduct religious services and welfare work.

'Men in working camps don't have time for recreation,' he said. 'Germany has been working like this for years as she is not such a rich country as England. That is what this war is all about.' It seemed that he saw me as another potential worker for Germany.

Sarcasm

Then his voice became more conciliatory with perhaps a touch of sarcasm. 'You are a Salvation Army captain,' he said. 'Salvation Army principles include willingness to do humble jobs.' At least he knew something about The Salvation Army. I replied that as a chaplain and welfare officer I was prepared to work only on behalf of fellow prisoners-of-war.

He looked thoughtful, and then continued, 'There are two alternatives. I must either give you a pass to go anywhere you like without a guard, or send you back to Stalag 4B.' A pause, his eyes met mine. 'No, I can't allow you to go without a guard. You might be undertaking espionage work.' He instances an occasion when French priests had helped men to escape.

Sermon

He eventually hit on a compromise. 'I must send English-speaking guards with you to listen to your sermon. As I am short of staff I will permit you to visit only at the weekends.'

For the rest of the time I would be incarcerated in the top floor room for five days of the week. I must have covered many miles during the next 16 months walking up and down that room. The only variation would be provided by the deaths of prisoners necessitating a midweek journey to conduct the funerals.

'Your first visit will be to a lead mine,' said the colonel. 'You will submit your sermon to me in duplicate by tomorrow morning.' Six sheets of paper were thrust towards me.

I thanked the colonel, remembered to click my heels and left the office. At the same time a prisoner, charged with threatening a German guard, was led in for sentence. He got 14 days 'bread and water'.

Spire

On my way out I met two Dutchmen who had been brought in having escaped twice, the second time reaching within sight of their village church spire. For many years after the war I corresponded regularly with one of these men. The Dutchmen sharing our 'League of Nations' building were fine representatives of their country. At meal times they always bowed their heads and said grace.

Two days later my guard/interpreter who was to accompany me to the lead mine at Freiburg appeared at 5.30 am with a cup of tea for me. With a haversack of hymn-books across my shoulder and my accordion in my left hand, I left my sleeping comrades and was soon walking briskly towards

Hartmannsdorf railway station with my compulsory companion.

Stomach

I felt sorry for this friendly middle-aged former schoolmaster as he poured out his troubles. Holding his stomach, he remarked, 'I have gastric ulcers and a lot of discomfort.' Then, a few yards further along the road, 'If only we had our colonies back we would be satisfied!'

At Freiburg we hunted for a suitable hotel where he could stay the night. He was unwilling to risk his health sleeping in the lead mine. Then we turned towards the slag heaps and the winding gear of the mine.

Two hundred prisoners worked there in appalling conditions – one wash-tap between them. All day they worked in wet conditions in the mine, only to return to damp huts where they slept. Seeing me looking at the line of washing strung across the hut, the corporal commented, 'That's been there for two weeks, and it's still not dry.'

Service

Most of the men suffered from rheumatism, and I wonder now what long-term effects those conditions had upon their health.

The guards treated them reasonably well, but the civilian bosses, who were fanatical Nazis, attacked them with rifle butts when they protested. Although attendance at the religious service was optional, every man was present.

I left the camp with the determination that, on arrival back at Hartmannsdorf, I would protest about the conditions in which these men lived and worked.

CHAPTER FORTY-ONE
Body Search

'THERE'S no Cypriot body here.' The old sexton in charge of the cemetery stood with the palms of his gnarled hands towards me seeming to say, 'Search me if you like.'

Someone must be crazy, I thought. The body could not have disappeared into thin air.

During the two-mile walk from Hohenstein Hospital the British prisoners, themselves recovering from various illnesses, recounted how the Cypriot had died from malnutrition. The hospital was in my 'parish' and I had travelled to Hohenstein for the funeral.

Although it was bitterly cold and the snow continued to fall, one of the Germans commented, 'At least it's better than the Russian front!'

Alternative

Suddenly the sexton had an idea. 'Come with me,' he said, like a salesman offering an alternative product. He swung open the door of a vault, revealing a coffin with the word 'Hollander' chalked on the side. 'Are you sure it is not a Dutchman you have come to bury?' he inquired. I explained that I was responsible for the funerals of members of the British Commonwealth only.

A tool-shed offered us shelter from the driving snow as we waited. I wondered how many more of these pilgrimages I would be called upon to make. Each journey to the cemetery meant grief for another family across the sea. Soon a Mum and Dad in Cyprus would hear news of their great loss.

Triangular

'The body has probably been mislaid in the hospital,' decided the sexton, going off to telephone. It was some time before he returned. He beckoned us to follow him.

We found ourselves inside a dirty, ill-kept building. If the outside bore some resemblance to a chapel, the inside dispelled such an impression. A long, narrow, triangular box rested on the floor.

'But where is the coffin?' I thought. A bell began to toll and my very kind guard, Morgenyer, whispered, 'Commence the service.' The narrow triangular box was the missing coffin.

After a short service, the British burial party carried the coffin down the sloping side of the cemetery to the grave. The shrill notes from the British bugle sounded over the snow. 'Fire!' shouted the German corporal as five German rifles fired a volley into the air.

As heads were bowed, I prayed, then read from the Scriptures and pronounced the committal. Even the name of the Cypriot soldier was unknown to me. His body had for a time been lost. But he was known and loved by God.

I never met the Cypriot in my life. Maybe I shall meet him in Heaven.

Within a few days I set out on a similar mission. An allied direct hit on an air-raid shelter had resulted in the death of three British prisoners of war.

Mixed with sorrow there was a sense of pride as I watched the British soldiers line up smartly. Members of the tank regiment, wearing black berets, were in front, the remainder following behind.

'Parade, by the left, quick march!' shouted the very efficient camp leader, Corporal Woods. As one man they marched with dignity through the streets of Niederwieza watched by local townspeople.

Memorial

After the service in the local church we made our way slowly to the graveyard. Our prisoners lined up on one side of the grave, the German firing party lined up on the other side, with German civilians. The three lads were buried side by side in a large grave as we committed their bodies to the ground and their eternal souls to God.

It was the last time I was to hear a German firing party at a British soldier's funeral. Because of the parlous condition of the nation, all leave was to be stopped and no bullets would be expended on burial firing parties.

The following Sunday I conducted the memorial service of the three lads in the camp.

CHAPTER FORTY-TWO
Chip Pans and Poems in a Storm

AN Anglican chaplain, bearing my surname, arrived at Hartmannsdorf Prison about six months after my arrival. I learned that we were to share the duties of visiting camps at weekends.

Richard Hill had been in officers' POW camps where the conditions were far superior to camps for 'other ranks'. We shared a two-tier bunk in the many solitary hours cooped up on the fifth floor.

With a mixture of excitement and apprehension Richard set off to the lead mine at Freiberg while I travelled in the opposite direction. Returning late on Sunday evening we happened to meet at Chemnitz Station.

Knowing Freiberg was a bad camp, I was not surprised to learn that the German under-officer had threatened to wreck Richard's service if it took more than three-quarters of an hour. Three men had recently escaped and so all camp entertainment had been forbidden.

Bannister

On arrival back we groped our way to our Red Cross box, endeavouring not to wake our 16 comrades. We then crept towards the dim light on the landing, sat on the stairs and in hushed voices swopped yarns about the day.

We dug into our box for morsels of hoarded food, while phantom-like figures making their way to the toilet brushed past us. Those with nothing on their feet glided by stealthily. Others, in heavy POW clogs, clattered along, probably holding on to the bannisters.

Culture

Richard Hill was a gracious personality, possessing the marks of true Christian culture. Once we managed to secure some potatoes which provided our evening meal for several days. Each evening, concealed behind some greatcoats hung for the purpose, I placed my frying-pan on a clandestine electric cooker.

The Germans knew that some electrical gadgets existed, for suddenly a fuse would blow. Then would follow a raid as we quickly smuggled the cookers to other hiding places.

As lightning flashed and rain splashed against the windows, I placed my pan of potatoes on the table and called, 'Richard, the potatoes are ready.' I confess that the pan of chips was the boundary of my vision.

Imagination

With a writing pad and pencil in hand, and with the imagination of a poet, Richard however stood motionless at the window. Soon on the pad appeared a poem, transforming that dreary storm into something exciting.

It was an illustration of the often quoted lines: 'Two men looked through prison bars, One saw mud and the other saw stars.'

Some years later I met Richard Hill again at Shrewsbury; he was then Rector of Berrington. As we drove out to the rectory we passed an imposing statue which reminded me of Nelson's Column. I remarked, 'Who's the old fellow stuck on top of that column?'

Connections

Imagine my surprise when Richard said, quite casually, 'As a matter of fact, that is a great-, great-, great-, (I forget the exact number of "greats") uncle of mine.

Apparently he was a general who fought with Wellington's army. It was typical of Richard Hill that during the whole time we lived together as prisoners-of-war, he had never once breathed a word about his distinguished family connections.

THE THUNDER STORM

(Richard Hill, Hartmannsdorf, July 3, 1944)

The thunder rolls vibrating through the sky
And shakes with pond'rous crash the breathless air:
The lightning runs its jagged course on high,
Its dazzling flashes mocking man's bold stare.

And now, the rain in hissing torrents falls,
Its solid streams beat down on road and roof,
Till gutters choke and splutter down the walls
Cascades of water, laughing at reproof.

The roadside stream is rising now apace
And races down its course, a muddy brown,
As drains and outfalls, set at frequent space,
Bring in their contribution from the town.

But pipes and culverts can no longer cope
With swirling floods that scorn such narrow ways
And rush in headlong course, as if they hope
To drown the world, as once in bygone days.

Across the road the muddy torrent flows,
Rejoicing in its freedom now achieved,
And joins the frothing stream as on it goes
Tumultuous with tribut'ries received.

At length the furious, gloomy storm rolls past,
The sun again dispels unnatural night,
The pelting rain subsides and stops at last,
Allowing the drenched village some respite.

And now the eager children all run out
To wade and frolic in the rushing brook;
Tremendous fun it is to splash and shout
Unchecked by any disapproving look.

Their energy spills out in glad release,
So long immured indoors because of rain:
Their previous boredom served but to increase
Their happiness now they are free again.

So when at last the clouds of war depart
And banished peace once more assumes her sway
A saddened world will bravely take fresh heart
And, smiling after tears, turn out to play.

CHAPTER FORTY-THREE
The Friendly Guard

IT was four o'clock on Sunday morning that my new guard came. A few whispered words were exchanged as I adjusted my haversack containing hymn books and a wooden cross. I gripped my accordion and left 18 sleeping comrades to their dreams.

My new guard introduced himself as Morgenyer and informed me that we were to visit a coal mine at Lukau. Before being conscripted into the army he had been a schoolteacher. At first I was a bit suspicious of his friendliness. Was he a stooge wanting to win my confidence to gain information about possible clandestine operations in the prison camps?

'No, thank you,' I replied, when he offered to help carry my accordion as we walked to the railway station. For a moment we walked in silence in the pitch darkness of the early morning.

'What a pity our two countries are both fighting each other,' he said, as we waited for our train to arrive. 'Why are there such things as wars and why does God allow it?' He spoke with such sincerity that I found my initial suspicion and resistance melting away.

Trouble

It soon became obvious that he wanted the journey to be a happy occasion. But there was a moment when his friendliness landed him in trouble.

I was relaxing in the railway carriage, looking at the

scenery and listening to his running commentary on the beautiful countryside.

'Look there,' he pointed with his finger, 'that is an ancient castle.' Then he fairly jumped out of his skin as a stern voice on his left commanded, 'It is forbidden to show landmarks to a prisoner.' It was the voice of a Nazi party man who had entered our carriage at the last station.

Poor Morgenyer went red with embarrassment. He shut up like a clam and remained silent for the rest of the journey.

'The British prisoners are not yet awake,' said the German under-officer when we arrived at the prison camp. They were probably exhausted from their long stint working down the mine.

'Let's go for a walk,' whispered Morgenyer, not wishing to stay around. About a mile from the prison camp, and after cautiously ensuring there were no observers, Morgenyer slapped me on the back in a friendly manner and said, 'Englishman, I am very happy to be with you today.'

Tunic

As we sat on the bank of a small river he took from his inside tunic pocket some photographs. 'That is my wife and children,' he said, passing me one of the pictures. 'And here are some snaps taken in England. I went on a Christian fellowship holiday to the Lake District,' his eyes shining with happy recollection. 'The people were so kind to me in England.'

He was obviously a very uncomplicated happy family man who lived for his wife and children. He wouldn't have made a soldier in thousand years; he was kind and considerate, and didn't even look comfortable in a soldier's uniform. Later in the day, when we were about to leave the coal-mine prison camp, I gave him a gentle nudge and said, 'Mr Morgenyer, you've got your hat on back to front.'

'Thanks,' he said, chuckling to himself.

On another of our journeys together we passed some children shrieking with delight as they slid downhill on a sledge. Morgenyer smiled, gave a quick glance at me, and we both joined in the fun – ending up snow-balling with the children.

On one occasion Morgenyer was particularly distressed. During one of the lightning searches at the Hartmannsdorf Camp the sum of £5 was found in my possession and confiscated by another guard when Morgenyer was acting as interpreter.

'If only you had given me the money before the search,' he said, 'I could have returned it to you afterwards.'

Turnout

Back at the coal mine we found a large crowd of men gathered for the service. Although attendance at religious services was optional, at most camps the turnout was usually 100 per cent.

After placing a wooden cross on the table at the front and distributing the hymn books, I asked the lads for their choice of hymns. Among the top favourites were 'Holy, holy, holy, Lord God Almighty!' 'When comes the promised time when war shall be no more', and 'The King of love my Shepherd is'. They were hymns many of them remembered singing at school assembly or Sunday-school.

Not many of them would have been regular attenders at church, but most had grown up with some belief in a God who cared, and to whom they were accountable for their actions. Some behaviour was right whereas other behaviour was definitely wrong. It made sense of life and gave to young people a feeling of emotional and spiritual security, self worth and confidence.

In contrast, present-day young people have been conned

and let down. They have been deprived of emotional and spiritual security, and many suffer a feeling of emptiness and a lack of identity.

'It will be a privilege to take part,' said Morgenyer, when I asked him if he would read the Bible in the service. Enemies discover a natural affinity when they both acknowledge Jesus Christ as the controlling influence in their lives.

It had been a happy day, I thought, as we arrived back at Hartmannsdorf late that night. 'Thanks for all your help, Mr Morgenyer, and give this to your children from me,' I said, handing him a bar of chocolate from my Red Cross parcel.

'Thanks,' he said, 'and I hope I can come with you again.' He did, on a number of occasions. When I eventually returned to England I sent his family a parcel of food.

CHAPTER FORTY-FOUR
The Guard who Collected Fag-ends

OF all my English-speaking German guards, the most comical – yet the most pathetic – was the 'Yank', so nick-named because of his American accent.

He was about 60. His scruffy uniform always had gaping seams or missing buttons. His two eyes appeared to operate independently, one eye coping with everyday affairs, while the other seemed to have X-ray powers to locate a discarded cigarette under a pile of rubbish. It would roam around until riveted by the sight of a fag-end. This would call forth either a wild yell of delight, or a sleight-of-hand trick so that the cigarette-end joined many others in the lining of Yank's pocket.

Typical of our journeys was one to Mumsdorf. As we set out Yank was apologetic about his conduct of the previous day. Entering our room drunk, he had used some vile language. He hastened to explain the circumstances: he had met a friend crying bitterly, having heard that his son had died on the Russian front. The two of them decided to drown their sorrows.

At Chemnitz, where we changed trains, I followed my guard to a little office at one end of the platform. In response to a knock on the door, his daughter appeared, kissed the old man and held out her hand for a small parcel.

He afterwards told me that the parcel contained stale bread which he had scrounged from friends. The girl would take this home for the family.

The industrial town of Chemnitz had a strange attraction

for the Yank, and we were soon walking its streets. At one time his family had owned a factory. Sometimes he gave me a colourful account of how he had been tricked out of the inheritance. I wondered whether beer and wild living had been the real cause.

Toothy

He made straight for a furrier's shop in the better-class part of the town. After acknowledging a toothy welcome from a stuffed bear, and running the gauntlet of suspended horns and antlers, we arrived at the counter. From the self-conscious grins of the two young lady assistants, I gathered the Yank was known to them.

One assistant fetched the manageress. An object in her hand was obviously the reason for our being there. I later discovered that she was one of Yank's contacts. She had known the family in better days, and because of that was one of Yank's regular benefactors.

Courtesy demanded some minutes of conversation. I was described as a 'Salvation Army clergyman'. Gracious goodbyes were offered and the object changed hands. The Yank left the shop a happy man with a handful of cigarette-ends plus a cigar.

At a hardware store and grocer's shop a similar procedure was repeated. At one he received only a cigar, at the other, in addition to cigarette-ends, some money.

In the previous week I had given him some of my German black sausage. Now he asked several times about my present-day ration, as we visited the camp on my programme and returned via Leipzig.

The Yank was either eating or talking, but not a pretty sight when trying to do both. His few loose false teeth entwined in his meat, resembling the action of a concrete-mixer. In the railway carriage he gave up the struggle with a piece of gristle, took from his pocket a paper bag and said to the lady sitting opposite, 'I'll take this home to my dog!'

Pathetic

He then continued his usual muddled conversation: 'Yes, I think the war will last another year. Ah! Churchill should be hanged. If you could give me a cigarette I should be all right. There are a lot of things you in England know nothing about. I feel better after the cup of tea they gave me at the camp.' And so on.

I grew to like poor old Yank. Perhaps he was most pathetic near the end of the war. Speaking out of a disillusioned heart as we stood on a railway station, he said, 'I'll never believe anything they tell me again.'

CHAPTER FORTY-FIVE
A Lesson in Contentment

'WAIT a minute,' I shouted, 'my coat is caught in the barbed wire.'

'OK, we've got the accordion,' said a voice from the darkness.

I let go of the accordion-case handle and released my coat from the barbed-wire fence. I jumped and found myself in a crowd of British prisoners, all eager to learn the latest war news and the fate of comrades in other camps.

Piltzer, my guard, followed me over the barbed-wire fence. He saw the funny side. 'Fancy climbing over a barbed-wire fence to get into a prison camp!' he said. 'I've heard of prisoners climbing a barbed-wire fence to get *out*, but not to get *in*.'

We had arrived at the camp about 15 minutes previously. Piltzer produced the documents authorising me to conduct a religious service.

But there was a snag. The camp guard who met us looked anxious. 'I can't find the key to open the door,' he explained. 'Perhaps my relief guard has taken it with him,' he said, gazing up at the ten feet high wall of barbed-wire fence. Then he added, 'Wait a minute.'

Slid down
Suddenly a cheer went up from the group of prisoners on the inside, as they watched their guard struggling to the barbed-wire fence with a long ladder. For a moment we watched as it see-sawed on the top of the fence, then slid

down to where we were waiting. So that was how we entered the prison camp when the guard couldn't find the key.

The 50 prisoners were packed into one small room. Festooned the length of the room was the prisoners' laundry, which had refused to dry in three weeks.

As soon as the service was over, we climbed the barbed wire again and walked through a forest to the nearest railway station.

Piltzer whistled German airs and I pulled the sledge on which rested my accordion. It had been Piltzer's idea to bring the sledge to transport the accordion. I appreciated the kind thought.

Piltzer was a tall, slim, fine-looking German. He had an air of authority and dignity, without any trace of arrogance. I came to respect him as a man of character. He was very patriotic, with a great love for his country, yet, in his heart, hated the Nazi philosophy.

An Allied bullet had found a place in his stomach, and secured him the position of interpreter and guard at a German prisoner-of-war camp. Much of his time was spent censoring letters. He spoke faultless English which sometimes sounded like a page from Shakespeare.

Caught up

On our return journey Piltzer confided that he had once been a candidate for the Lutheran ministry. On arrival at Chemnitz there was no train connection, so we set out on a two-hour walk.

Along the road we caught up with an old lady carrying a heavy bundle. Piltzer relieved her of the burden. She had lost all her possessions in the bombing of Chemnitz, she told us, and was now on her way to the home of friends outside the town. We spoke in a strictly neutral manner of the frightfulness of war, with its accompanying tragedies.

The snow crunched beneath our feet as we trudged back to camp. Piltzer opened up about the plight of his own family. His father was a university professor. 'My parents are now living in a cellar,' he said, 'and all they possess is one hundred marks and a sack of potatoes.'

Then, speaking out of the fullness of his faith, he said, 'I shall always remember the Scripture you read in the service tonight: "I have learned, in whatsoever state I am, therewith to be content'."*

Jesus Christ was reigning in the citadel of his soul. No tragedy could overwhelm him.

*Philippians 4:11, Authorised Version

CHAPTER FORTY-SIX
The Guard who Took me Home

'DON'T speak to me,' whispered my guard. 'Just walk before me and do what I do.'

I followed him along a road in Chemnitz. My guard on this occasion was a member of the Nazi party. Although he held no high rank, the other guards, not party members, appeared uneasy in his presence and even afraid.

Earlier in the day we had visited two camps in the Chemnitz area. At one I met the South African camp leader nicknamed 'Zulu Brown'. There was a spirit of caring in his camp. He looked after his men, buried them, conducted services, and even managed to get some dying American prisoners transferred to his camp, so saving their lives.

As we walked through the devastated remains of Chemnitz, civilians were salvaging what remained of their homes after the bombing. My guard had explained that all leave for German soldiers had been cancelled. As a member of the Nazi party he had manipulated this journey, to nip home for an hour when we changed trains at Chemnitz.

Gestapo

But what could he do with me? As neither the Gestapo nor the police would be responsible for me, he had decided to take me home with him. This member of the party would break the rule forbidding prisoners in one's home.

I followed him up several flights of stairs to a top flat. It was about three years since I last entered a home. A slim, pleasant lady dressed in black opened the door.

In perfect English she said, 'May I offer you my hand, Englishman?' She smiled, and then explained, 'My husband rang up and said he was bringing a clergyman home. I imagined a benign old gentleman with a beard.'

I was 23 years old!

I sat down to tea in the beautiful Nazi home, graciously accepted another biscuit and became aware of the lady's gaze on my shoulder insignia. She exclaimed, 'Salvation Army! But you look all right.'

'Thank you,' I replied, 'but why are you surprised?'

'Well, you are like my own two sons, and I could never imagine them belonging to The Salvation Army.'

'Tell me about your image of The Salvation Army,' I said.

'My only knowledge is of funny people on street corners playing guitars!'

After tea my guard, who had business matters to deal with, went to his office.

'You have not seen the inside of a home for a long time,' the lady said. 'Perhaps you would care to see our home.'

The furnishings indicated that this was not a poor man's home. I looked at the modern equipment in the kitchenette, and remarked on the comfort of it all.

The lady was overcome and tears began to flow. 'I used to love to make it nice for my two boys, but now I don't care. My boys have been killed on the Russian front.'

Here was great sorrow. She had no personal knowledge of Jesus Christ who said, 'I am the resurrection, and the life,' and 'Lo, I am with you alway'.*

*John 11:25; Matthew 28:20, Authorised Version

The feeling of despair came to me as I walked the streets of the big towns. Slave labour was everywhere; old women doing heavy manual work under appalling conditions. It was depressing and revolting. Some of the Germans could see that their country was fast becoming morally bankrupt. As I looked into the faces of those living under such soulless conditions, it seemed that all light had gone from their eyes. Something within them had died.

CHAPTER FORTY-SEVEN
Not Exactly a Barrel of Fun

AN unusual sound – a barrel-organ! I went to the window on the fifth floor, and the little stream running beside the village street seemed to dance in time with the music.

An old man in a peaked cap churned out the music. He looked up, smiled and waved his cap to acknowledge the few pfennigs I threw out of the window. Then the village of Hartmannsdorf was treated to the strains of 'Roll out the barrel, we'll have a barrel of fun'.

I waved goodbye and thought, 'Not exactly a barrel of fun here.' Like a caged animal I walked 20 paces to the end of the room followed by 20 to the other. How many times had I done that? I would read until my eyes were tired, then pace the room, then read – and so it went on, five days each week, sometimes six.

That was my weekly programme for 16 months until the Americans captured the village.

Once my walking ritual was suddenly interrupted when the door was thrust open. 'You must stop this,' said the German figure in the doorway. 'We are trying to work on the floor below, but you are disturbing our concentration.'

'But I have no opportunity to exercise,' I replied, 'apart from the weekends when I visit other camps.'

Half-an-hour later an elderly guard appeared. 'I have come to escort you around the village and across the fields,' he explained.

'Wonderful!' I said, reaching for my Salvation Army cap. 'Is this to be every day?'

'No, just one hour once a week.'

Relief

Still, that was better than nothing. What a relief to be outside, with country lanes and fields before me! Like a greyhound let loose from the trap I was off, swinging my arms and whistling, 'Roll out the barrel!'

But not for long. 'Slowly, more slowly!' pleaded my guard, holding his chest to indicate that some part of his body was sick.

At about 6 pm each day my fellow-prisoners would return from their working party. They were a lively lot, although prisoner-of-war life was beginning to affect some of them. It was a joke among us that you could tell how long a person had been a prisoner by how far he had gone 'round the bend'.

Sammy, a former dancer, was the wit of the party. In a particularly happy mood he would grab hold of one of our guards and dance with him round the room.

Razor

For Eggy – so called because of his bald head – POW life was having a bad effect. He could spend a whole evening looking into a mirror, holding a safety razor. He would experiment with facial gymnastics, then gently apply the razor to one part of his face. After a long pause there would be more face-pulling and another scrape. His only other interest was reckoning up his post-war credits.

Vicky was a fanatical communist. 'When everyone has equality, and economic security,' he would argue, 'all evil such as stealing will disappear. Man will no longer have any need or desire to steal.' Apparently Christianity would become a museum piece rendered redundant.

I sometimes wonder what Vicky thinks now. I still believe

there is such a thing as original sin. Although it is God's plan that we should all reach our full potential as human beings, man prevents this by his self-will. It is tragically possible that we can simply drift through this life without ever discovering life's true meaning.

CHAPTER FORTY-EIGHT
Time to Confess

'WE would like to make our confessions. Can you help us?'

Two devout Roman Catholics were to stay overnight at the Hartmannsdorf prison, *en route* for another working camp. Hartmannsdorf was often used as a transit camp, as well as housing prisoners awaiting trial for offences against the Reich. These were locked up on the top floor.

How could I help these men? I was the only chaplain for the 80 British working camps, and no Catholic chaplain existed. But prison life had taught me to be resourceful. 'Just give me a few minutes,' I said reassuringly.

I descended to the fourth floor to the workroom where a prisoner in French uniform was huddled over a bench. 'Good morning, father,' I said, as the small shy man greeted me with a smile. 'I want your help.' British Army chaplains ranked as officers, but French priests were, in the main, not given that status. Therefore, as prisoners of war they were required to work, and didn't have the privilege of visiting other prison camps to conduct services.

'I would like to help the British prisoners, but,' – he knocked out his pipe – 'I don't speak English.' It was his turn to appeal for help. 'Will you translate for me?'

Barriers

My mind worked fast on two levels. Firstly, denominational barriers fell down in prison camps. If the confession was to help these men, the fact that I held different theological views was insufficient reason to withhold help. However, my vivid imagination conjured up disastrous consequences arising from my limited knowledge of the language. Recently a French prisoner had playfully said of my French, 'You speak French like a Spanish cow!' I might confess the wrong sins, and the men could end up doing penance for the rest of their lives. Still, in the prison camp was a French sergeant-major, Guy Ferron, a devout Roman Catholic, who spoke better English than I did French. Yes, he would gladly act as translator. Guy became a personal friend and I correspond with him to this day.

Complaints

By obtaining the help of others I had met the needs of these two prisoners. But I must confess to being a failure with the next request.

We had now been prisoners of war for about two-and-a-half years. The British camp leader told me there had been complaints by other prisoners that two men had been observed cuddling and kissing each other on a top bunk.

Here was the first case of homosexuality I had ever come across. In today's sexual climate people might imagine that during those years thousands of men, denied the usual sexual outlets, would be engaging in regular homosexual orgies. It was not so. Like myself, many would know nothing about homosexuality.

From the age of 14 to 18 years I had worked in factories and on building sites, observing crude horseplay from time to time. Yet homosexual practices were unknown to me. How different it is today!

How did I deal with the situation?

I didn't. I hadn't a clue. To order them to stop it when I didn't even understand it seemed futile. But ignorance prevented me from being of help.

Tendencies

I was a spiritual leader and should have known how to help. I was challenged, and had to make good this gap in my understanding, as well as discover what the Bible teaches about it.

Since those days I have spent considerable time as a counsellor talking with people with homosexual tendencies. I have learned that one cannot put a neat label on them. Every such person is an individual; what homosexuality means to one is different from what it means to another.

CHAPTER FORTY-NINE
Night in the Punishment Cell

'THE old man is looking quite a sight,' I thought as I glanced at my guard trudging beside me. The holes in 'Yank's' trousers and his threadbare tunic seemed to defy needle and cotton. It must have been a long time since he had had a new uniform.

In contrast I was wearing a new battle-dress recently received from the Red Cross. It was good to feel smart after more than two years in odd clothing.

Soon Yank's acquisitive eye spied a rag doll in the gutter. Like a hunting dog, the Yank sprang into action.

'It's useless,' I remonstrated, 'better left where it is.'

But Yank continued to the station, his rifle over one shoulder, the rag doll in his other hand.

During my journeys with Yank, he revealed the range of his emotions. He could be happy, laughing, sad, scrounging for cigarettes, drunk, swearing, hating the world for the misfortunes inflicted on him, and yet possessing a childlike naivety. I found him vulnerable and likeable.

The station platform was packed on the first stage of our weekend journey to visit camps. I was no authority on railway engines, but I was sure this one should not have emitted steam from so many places.

The carriage were crammed, but the station official simply started at one end of the train, opened each door and forced two more people inside. I was pushed into one carriage and my guard into another.

148

Haversack

An hour later I heard shouts from the next carriage. 'Captain Hill, we get out at this station!'

'Excuse me,' I said, making a grab at my haversack on the rack. The haversack disgorged an avalanche of hymns – ancient and modern – on the lady sitting underneath!

In the delightful town of Weissenfelds, women were doing their Saturday shopping. We walked by the river, which reminded me of the Thames at Chertsey, crossed a bridge and arrived at a little general store. I was offered lemonade by the lady of the house - who gave a dramatic account of recent bombing raids which had wiped out a local oil factory.

Celebration

As we walked towards the working camp, Yank - still clutching the doll – gave me his amended views of the war. 'Everything is in a mess,' he said. 'The Almighty should come and get us out of it.'

My arrival at the camp was an occasion of celebration and reunion. Most were lads I had known in Italian prison camps. There was a spirit of optimism. The news was good; the Allies had landed in France and a speedy end to the war was anticipated.

I was to lead a service the next morning, but tonight a social evening had been arranged.

Accordion

A curtain was rigged up for what was called a radio play. The cast read their parts behind the curtain. Then, accompanied by my accordion, the 83 men sang lustily all their favourite songs.

But as the singing ended, men began to remove their boots and trousers and place them in the centre of the hut. A guard carried them off. Apparently it was to prevent attempts to escape.

'Your trousers and boots, too!' demanded the guard.

'We can give them spare ones,' whispered a British sergeant. But I refused to comply, preferring to protest in order to help other prisoners. So I was led off to the guardroom.

On his return Yank was genuinely distressed. 'I can't intervene because the camp guard is of higher rank.'

So I was led to the underground punishment cell as the guardroom radio announced the approach of British planes over the area. Two blankets were thrown to me and I was soon asleep.

I awoke cold and dirty to the opportunities of another Sunday, and emerged into the sunlight. The lads had arranged the chairs for the service and my wooden cross was at the front. We were soon praising God for his protecting care.

On my return to Hartmannsdorf I reported the incident. The senior German officer gave me a written statement that I must not again be treated in that way.

CHAPTER FIFTY
Looking for Hope

'IF I had a gun,' said Bill, glaring angrily at the crowd of Germans on the railway platform, 'I'd shoot the lot of you!'

This ginger-haired, powerfully built American turned on our embarrassed German guard. 'Yes, you as well.' With his blood at boiling point he was like a man possessed, fearing nothing and nobody.

I placed a restraining hand on his arm. 'Careful, Bill.' I was uncomfortably aware that we were becoming the focus of attention.

In his present mood Bill was ready to take on the whole German nation including Hitler. It was as if something had snapped and he was not responsible for his actions. As the situation became more tense, I could see us being lynched. It was a merciful relief when our train pulled into the station and Bill was bundled into the railway compartment.

What had sparked off Bill's outburst? Earlier that day he had been incensed by appalling conditions in a prison camp housing American prisoners. The Allied landing in Europe, and the entrance of America into the war, had added the camp to my list of weekly visits. Bill had been selected as the American 'man of confidence' to accompany me on my first visit.

Here was the picture which met us.

Presence
The sight of a dead body of an American soldier lying on the coals at the entrance to the former beer house did not

augur well. I should have been informed of his death and conducted his funeral.

'They don't look like Americans,' said Bill, pointing towards the listless groups who appeared not to register our presence. 'They look more like ghosts.' They seemed past caring. From three-tier bunks came moans as if the occupants were ill.

As no preparation had been made for the service, I placed my bag of hymn books and accordion on the floor and grasped the nearest form.

'Come on, you fellows! You're dying like flies. Get to this service!' shouted a fellow who introduced himself as the camp leader. Gradually those not too ill shuffled towards us and took their places.

'Choose your own hymns,' I said, handing out the hymn books. A former medical student sat at a grand piano, left behind by the landlord of the beer house.

If only I could describe the unique atmosphere of that occasion! A sprinkling of negroes looked at me from the congregation. I thought that black faces looked even more sad than the white ones. Their thin faces, eyes appearing larger than usual, looked wistfully for some comfort and hope.

The piano began the tune 'Toplady'. Then the prisoners lifted their hearts and voices as they sang:

Rock of ages, cleft for me,
Let me hide myself in thee.

The pianist played as one inspired. It seemed that I had never heard such music. God came very near as sadness and exquisite beauty blended. Like Christ on the cross, here was suffering and victory, defeat and triumph.

Pianist

Could they have another service tomorrow, they asked

eagerly, not realising how far I had travelled. Could someone else be sent from HQ to be their camp leader?

From the pianist I learned that a number of men had died recently. I had not been notified and no Christian burials had been performed. The bodies had been simply taken out of the camp.

The pianist also told me of his hopes for a medical career. He produced a photograph of the lovely girl waiting for him in America, wiped away a tear with his grimy yet artistic hand, and said, 'I'll never be able to ask her to marry me now. Since coming here I have developed a bad heart.'

He paused. 'Did you see the body outside? That was my pal. A few days before he died, some Red Cross food arrived. My pal was not so fortunate as some of the others when the cards were cut and the allocation made.

'He desperately wanted a pot of jam, to remind him of the kind his mother used to make. So he starved himself for three days, and bartered his three-day bread ration for a pot of jam.

'That night he went to sleep, clasping his jam. But when he awoke someone had stolen it. He became delirious, and was heard saying just before he died, "Never mind, I'll save up and buy another."'

It was this that had made Bill so upset and angry as we waited for the train to take us to the next camp.

CHAPTER FIFTY-ONE
Caught in an Air Raid

FROM the POW camp for Americans I went to Zeits to conduct a service with some South African prisoners. The camp leader there, nicknamed Zulu Brown, was a tall, fine-looking man who had once been on an expedition to the South Pole. He was an outstanding leader, dedicated to the welfare of his men, caring for them when they were sick and conducting their religious services.

It was a hurried visit. By 9 pm we were on Leipzig station. The next train to Chemnitz was at 4 am the following morning.

Though constantly castigated by Bill, my American companion, our guard was not a bad fellow. By profession a bank official, he possessed mastery of several languages. But he was not vivacious or colourful. He asked no more than to be quietly left alone. The prospect of a few hours with his wife in Leipzig made our guard quicken his step as we passed into the blackout conditions of the city.

Metal wheels clattering on rails grew to a crescendo and then stopped. 'Don't speak at all,' whispered our guard, shepherding us on the overcrowded tram. Prisoners were not allowed in trams; but it was dark and nobody knew who we were.

Everything was working to plan. Then the wail of the air-raid siren pierced the darkness.

'Quick, get to the shelter,' said the guard, the first part of his plan ruined. He had hoped to take us home under the cover of darkness.

The guard had to take us down into the cellar beneath the block of flats where his wife lived. We entered a clean, well-lit cellar used by the occupants of the flats as an air-raid shelter.

Gloating

It was strange to be dressed in British uniform, mingling with about 20 German civilians. Our common purpose was to avoid being the target of the British bombers. I tried to guess what the people's feelings might be. I had to be careful. To smile might be misunderstood as gloating; to appear too aloof might be regarded as arrogance.

An earnest, but pleasant-faced woman entered the cellar and carefully placed on the floor a bird cage and a wicker basket from which came an occasional 'Meow'. Our guard introduced the woman as his wife.

I stood by an alcove, trying to reveal no emotion, when a middle-aged German approached me.

'Englishman, don't stand there. You are more likely to be killed if the bomb falls near.' He smiled and pointed upward. 'I know they are your planes up there. But don't worry, I have nothing against you.'

Although I represented the enemy, I was accepted, forgiven. Early that morning at the American camp I had witnessed brutality, but now I was experiencing kindness.

Conversation ceased as a radio announcer was heard. 'Heavy formations flying towards square six.'

Everybody moved to where a map hung above the radio. My new German friend showed me the small numbered squares. We were number eight. The announcer came again: 'Light formations moving to square eight.'

We waited. Suddenly the ground shook. 'A near one,' commented my guard.

Strolling

As the 'all clear' sounded, my guard was anxious that no one must know that we would be in his flat. In the most ostentatious manner we said 'Good night' to our guard's wife, then to all the other occupants of the cellar, making sure that everyone saw us leave.

After strolling around for about 20 minutes we found ourselves back at the flats. 'Be very quiet,' cautioned the guard, as we made our way up four flights of stairs. Almost at our destination, my boots slipped and the stone steps re-echoed with a clatter which seemed to circle endlessly.

Soon we were inside. Bill, who earlier had threatened to shoot every German, produced some American coffee from his pocket and offered it to our guard's wife. We spent a very pleasant few hours drinking coffee and talking.

Usurping

The guard's wife was interested in spiritualism, which led us to discuss its benefits or dangers. I made the point that while spiritualism may point to the reality of a supernatural world, it should not become the centre of worship. Anything usurping the central place of Christ was wrong.

Our conversation came to an end only when the guard looked at the clock and reminded us that our train left at 4 am.

CHAPTER FIFTY-TWO
Brutality and Kindness

I WONDER what conditions will be like at this camp?' I often thought as I approached the barbed wire of another working camp. Conditions varied considerably. I was constantly shocked by the brutality and sometimes impressed by acts of kindness.

At Rohrsdorf the local Germans were most helpful. Thirty prisoners lived in a hut 20 feet by 24 feet. 'We are going to the local public-house for the service,' the British sergeant informed me.

Candles

'What lovely flowers!' I exclaimed, as the landlady of the little inn showed me into the room she had made beautiful for the occasion. And she had put a piano at our disposal.

More often than not, however, the service took place in the barracks. At one camp – where the Church of England representation was strong – the prisoners had built an altar, complete with candles.

Once I found myself in a tyre factory. 'You have only a quarter of an hour during the meal break,' said one of the German officials. I carried with me a wooden cross made by a French carpenter. I placed it on a pile of tyres in a corner of the yard. In the moments that followed we turned our thoughts to God and sang,

Holy Father, in thy mercy,
Hear our anxious prayer:

Keep our loved ones, now far distant,
'Neath thy care.

Sometimes several camps would combine for a service. At Freiburg I came across a company of prisoners marching through the streets to join their comrades at a combined service. In that camp conditions were particularly bad.

Conditions
I had authority for nothing other than conducting religious services. Nevertheless, when I came across bad treatment I reported it to headquarters. As a result conditions were occasionally improved.

At Schopau the guard commander appeared unreasonable; even when the daily quota of work was done, he would tell a prisoner to pick creeper off the barbed wire, or perhaps order a saluting parade. The headquarters commandant listened to my account and promised to investigate. The guard was removed from the camp.

In some camps I found flourishing Christian fellowships. I noticed men whose knowledge of spiritual things had developed during the Italian days. They were now leading services and Bible classes. I often returned to headquarters with notes such as: 'Werdun camp requires 20 hymn books; Zwickau needs 25.' When supplies were available I had them sent to the camps.

Of the thousands who died as prisoners of war or slaves in Germany, a good number of the corpses ended in lime pits. Yet on other occasions the utmost courtesy would be shown.

Crumbs
At a cemetery for the funeral of an American, I was met by a Dickensian character in a long black coat and top hat.

He removed breakfast crumbs from his mouth and escorted me to a beautiful chapel where the coffin lay draped with an American flag and surrounded by electric candles. As I pronounced the committal, refugees from the Eastern front passed by.

Creatures

On another occasion I went to Frankenburg where, in the corner of a church, a group of prisoners huddled together. It was bitterly cold.

Not since our Italian days had I seen such wretched creatures. They were thin and ill, and wore old Russian clothes. Holes were in their boots and they had no underclothing. Even my guard said he had not seen Englishmen in such a state. They were there to pay tribute to another member of their little camp, Matthew Orr, who came from Glasgow. It was with great difficulty that they carried the coffin to the grave.

Typical Prussian guards escorted them to the graveside. But there a woman sexton in uniform, complete with peak cap, handed to each prisoner a small bunch of flowers to throw on the coffin.

Chemnitz was a camp I liked. The guard there was like an old mother to the prisoners, worrying even if a button was off their coats. 'Can we have the chorus you taught us?' said one when I made my second visit. 'We sing it every morning,' said another. 'A fellow isn't properly initiated until he's learned it. We've even taught it to the guard,' he added.

The chorus was:

He careth for you, he careth for you.
In sunshine or shadow he careth for you.

CHAPTER FIFTY-THREE
Destruction

APRIL 1945 found the prisoners in a state of excitement. In the French room was a map of Europe with the front line marked by black pins. Each day the pins were moved nearer to our town.

The Russian army was galloping from the east and the Allied forces approaching from the west. Which would arrive first and what would happen? The worst rumour was that a last-ditch desperate stand would be made and all prisoners shot.

But from my observation this was unlikely as the Germans had very little fight left. On one journey I met two German soldiers from the Russian front. 'It is futile,' they said, 'because we've nothing to fight with. We dig gun pits but have no guns to put in them.'

When we parted company they insisted on shaking hands and wishing me the best of luck.

Not so long before it had seemed that every German was afraid of his neighbour lest he or she be reported for disloyalty. People now openly spoke of the impending doom. It was as if they didn't have feelings any more, but were stunned and shocked and mutely waiting for the end.

Smoke

Refugees from the cities constantly trudged through our village, their faces black from the smoke of burning Chemnitz. The town had come to a standstill. The trams remained where they had stopped at the time of the last air raid. The people were without bread and the water supply had ceased.

I met British prisoners clearing rubble. They told me that the bodies of two German soldiers had not been collected, whereas a horse's carcass had been removed immediately for food.

At night we witnessed the bombing of Chemnitz and Dresden. The sound overhead made it difficult to carry on a conversation. The sky was ablaze with light and the two towns shook. So many beautiful buildings were destroyed in Dresden including the cathedral, and the scarred statue of Martin Luther lay face down in the rubble, blasted 20 yards from its pedestal.

More people perished in Dresden than either Hiroshima or Nagasaki. Many claim that about 300,000 were killed, although the general consensus puts the figure at half that number. To aid identification more than 10,000 wedding rings were cut from bodies. German custom required the initials of the wearer to be engraved on the inside of the ring.

A crowd of Polish girls, mainly students, invaded our prison. They had been captured in Warsaw. It was strange to hear girls' voices in the building, and even stranger to hear one of them say, 'We had to give in. We had only two machine guns left.'

What courage! Yet they were so petite and ran about the building like little imps during their days with us.

A group of Jewish women being evacuated from a concentration camp in the east passed through our village. Many were without shoes and looked a pitiful sight. The police escort carried whips, and one woman had the side of her face slashed and bruised because she could not keep up.

April 13 arrived. An uneasy atmosphere was abroad. The same little stream flowed by the side of the road outside the prison, but it seemed to speak of events moving swiftly to a climax.

Otto Zelpman, a German officer whom we nicknamed 'Nutcracker', met me on the stairs. He belonged to a group of officers secretly opposed to the Nazi regime. This day he looked apprehensive.

'It's all over now,' he confided. 'They have removed all photos of Hitler from the office. I think your friends, the Americans, will be here by tonight.'

Poor old Zelpman! Little did he know what was to come. Later arrested by the Russians, he was given 25 years' penal servitude for crimes against humanity. He was to receive no news from his family for six years, and then to learn that his wife had committed suicide believing him to have disappeared for ever in Siberia.

Six years later I was to write him a testimonial certifying that he had treated us decently and, to my knowledge, had committed no crime.

Safety

That afternoon the distant sound of guns was heard. Piltzer came to tell me that the Americans were much nearer than even the BBC had announced.

Although our personal safety was in doubt, we couldn't help feeling sorry for some of our guards. Although prisoner-of-war life had been no picnic, we harboured no grudge or hatred towards them.

'Look at poor old Fritz down there,' exclaimed Sammy, pointing to the corner of the street where Fritz and his mate Titch were struggling with an ammunition box. 'If an American tank comes round the corner,' said Vicky, with genuine concern, 'poor old Fritz won't stand a chance.'

The next few hours would decide our fate.

CHAPTER FIFTY-FOUR
Freedom is Near

ALL night we sat listening to the Allied guns. Were they getting nearer, or was it my imagination? 'As soon as it is daylight,' said Bill, our expert on military strategy, 'they will break through and capture Hartmannsdorf.'

And then – at 4 am on 14 April, 1945, a German guard appeared. 'Get outside!' he bawled. We were to be marched further away from our liberators, to the Erzgebirge Mountains bordering Czechoslovakia. My mind did a quick flashback to our Italian prisoner-of-war days. We had been so near to freedom then, only to have it cruelly snatched away.

I looked lovingly at my accordion. It had done valiant service in the various camps. Regretfully I had to leave it behind. The prospect of marching, and of nights spent beneath the stars, meant that a blanket must take priority.

There was no moon and the pitch darkness matched our mood as we shuffled through Hartmannsdorf. 'Looks as if we're going to Leiber's,' said Sammy. Sure enough, we stopped at Leiber's, the warehouse where Red Cross parcels were stored for British prisoners. After each received a parcel, the 18 British prisoners were followed by hundreds of prisoners of other nationalities.

Once inside the building my eyes surveyed every possible hiding-place. A quick word with my friend, Chaplain Richard Hill, and I had disappeared.

This was no daring escape. I simply dropped down behind some packing-cases to await the entry of the Americans.

Guarded

Within an hour all prisoners had left – or so I thought – and the store was guarded by the German Home Guard. Dawn arrived, but no grand entry. If anything it seemed the gunfire had lessened.

At 11 am I decided to come out of my hiding-place. I imagined that the guard might leap at me with revolver drawn. On the contrary, as I reached the floor level he casually glanced at me. I felt rather self-conscious, picked up a broom and started to sweep the floor.

Within minutes other British prisoners began to reappear. Two heads popped out of a water tank. Soon the whole 18 of us were present.

About two hours later, sudden bursts of machine-gun fire – unhealthily close – sent us scurrying down a hole originally made for German soldiers. Once down the hole I decided that, having survived three years as a prisoner, I had no inclination to pop my head up until assured the battle was over.

Remained

While shells flew and rifles cracked, we remained in the dug-out, along with a German civilian and two little boys. With food from the Red Cross store, we fed the old man who ate it hungrily and declared he could do with more. The two boys ate chocolate and were quite excited about this 'war game'. We had to restrain them from popping their heads up to see how the battle was progressing.

At the end of an unusually long period of comparative calm I climbed above ground. From the windows of every house, white sheets, white pillow cases, anything white, were flying. The town had surrendered. A Frenchman told us that the town had fallen to the Americans.

The war for us was over, and we were released.

We were soon greeted by the Americans, who looked like small armament factories with all their arms and ammunition slung around them. Polish women occupants of a concentration camp nearby had also been released. They were starving, pitiful sights and were most grateful to receive the Red Cross food.

The town had been captured by the spearhead of an armoured division. The mopping-up operations had to await the coming of the infantry the next day.

That night the Americans entertained us right royally with steaks, green peas and potatoes. We slept at the Leiber's warehouse, the Americans mounting a guard for our protection.

The following day was regarded by all prisoners and forced labour workers as a bank holiday. If anyone had any best clothes they certainly wore them.

CHAPTER FIFTY-FIVE
Mixed Emotions

IT was about 5 pm when the American driver put his lorry into gear and we waved goodbye to fellow-prisoners of other nationalities.

I looked at the group of Russian prisoners who had suffered so much. No transport would be taking them back home. A long walk was before them.

The residents of Hartmannsdorf feared the approach of the Russian army and were almost relieved when the Americans captured their village. They did not know that very soon their part of Germany would be included in the Russian zone of East Germany.

The little stream which gurgled and splashed over the stones, had seen many changes since the village had fallen to the Americans 24 hours earlier. On our journey from the front line we witnessed the bodies of German soldiers not yet buried, and many burnt-out German vehicles. We were most grateful to the Americans for hastening our departure from the scene of action.

After three miles an American soldier pointed with his automatic weapon to a little hamlet in a valley. 'See those houses?' he said. 'Just go down and commandeer the place. If you have any trouble with the people we will come down and sort them out.'

Feeble attempt

It was about 6 pm when my fellow-chaplain Richard Hill and I, along with five other British prisoners, entered the yard of a modest farmhouse.

I am sure that our American friends would have been quite ashamed of our feeble attempt at being 'tough guys'. All male Germans in the area had been taken prisoner. A woman drawing water from the yard pump looked terrified. Instead of taking possession of the house, we approached apologetically and asked if we might be allowed to sleep in the barn for the night.

The lady's face registered relief when she realised we were not desperadoes. In order not to embarrass her we did not enter the house, but fried eggs and meat on a fire we built in the yard.

Later, a grandmother cautiously appeared, followed by two girls of about 10 and 15 years. The children accepted the chocolate we offered and the whole household began to relax. The sun was beginning to set when the mother invited us into the house for the evening.

Grandma lit the oil lamp, we shared our American food, and an old-fashioned accordion was produced from behind the sofa. We had a happy evening singing – and watching Bill, who came from the Elephant and Castle district of London, do some card tricks. Bill's patter in broken German was the most comical part of the act; the smaller girl shrieked with laughter. I am sure she had not experienced such a happy evening for a long time.

Would we like to remain in the home for the night? We thanked the mother for her kindness but assured her we would be perfectly comfortable in the barn.

We soon curled up in the straw with thoughts racing through our minds. Could it be true? Were we really free at last?

'Hope nobody comes and cuts our throats tonight,' said 'Eggy', who was probably still working out his post-war credits.

'Shut up and go to sleep!' said Sammy.

Next day, while travelling by lorry to a French airport, I began to experience a reaction – physical, emotional and mental.

Three years

After three years as a prisoner I no longer needed to assume moral and spiritual leadership. No longer must I maintain the spirit and morale of those around me. Some used to say, 'You seem to like this prison life.'

No more would I have to stand beside the coffin of a fellow-prisoner and pronounce the words of committal.

My friend Harold Barker had been an example and inspiration. Never once had I heard him inflict his own personal troubles, pains and distress on another person even though at times he was a very sick man. He lived near to the spirit of Jesus Christ and thought only of the welfare of others.

My thoughts and emotions were mixed. One part of me was terribly relieved that it was all over. Yet I could not escape the feeling that with the accumulated wisdom and experience of the past three years, I should like to go through it again, but do it all so much better. God had been good to me; He had taught me so much.

As the Dakota plane touched down at Cardington airstrip, it was as if all the pent-up emotions of the past three years were surfacing. Perhaps God was giving me permission to be weak, vulnerable and human.

I stood on the tarmac and the tears flowed.